*Paul's Comfort*

# Paul's Comfort

*Faith for an Extraordinary Life*

Volume 2

of

The Promises of God

Series

**Travis Toth**

**Paul's Comfort**

*Faith for an Extraordinary Life*

*Volume 2 of "The Promises of God" Series*

Second Edition Copyright © 2018 by Travis Toth. All rights reserved.

---

No part of this publication may be reproduced, stored in a retrieval system or transmitted in any way by any means, electronic, mechanical, photocopy, recording or otherwise without the prior permission of the author except as provided by USA copyright law.

All Scripture References Provided From: *The Holy Bible, New International Version®*, NIV® Copyright © 1973, 1978, 1984, 2011 by Biblica, Inc.® Used by permission. All rights reserved worldwide.

---

First and Second Editions Published in the United States of America

---

First Edition Published by Tate Publishing & Enterprises, LLC
First Edition book design copyright © 2015 by Tate Publishing, LLC. All rights reserved.
First Edition cover design by Bill Francis Peralta
First Edition interior design by GramTelen

Second Edition Published by Kindle Direct Press
Second Edition book design modified version of First Edition design
Second Edition cover design modified version of First Edition design
Second Edition interior design modified version of First Edition design

---

First Edition ISBN: 978-1-68164-661-9
1. Religion / Christian Life / Personal Growth
2. Religion / Christian Life / Spiritual Growth 15.08.04

---

Second Edition ISBN: 978-1-72409-066-9
1. Nonfiction / Religion / Christian Life / Personal Growth
2. Nonfiction / Religion / Christian Life / Spiritual Growth

# Dedication

I dedicate this book to Zachary, Elizabeth, and Daniel Toth, my precious gifts from God. In a world where nothing seems sacred anymore, and there is only a blurred vision of right and wrong, my little children give me hope and reason to fight. I have learned so much about God through their lives already, and I look forward to continuing to pour my life and the love of God into their hearts for many years to come.

There is nothing on this earth more valuable than the family, and nothing more precious to God than the family that prays together in Jesus's name. When Jill and I began our journey as parents, we heard it said many times that a parent's job is to point children in the right direction like an arrow. Likewise, that you should raise a child in the way he or she should go and when older, they will not depart from the ways of God.

However, I have learned that the most important part a parent can play is to pray: pray and petition God for their salvation. Instead of hoping they become saved, pray and declare it so, and God will answer the petition of your heart. Only then can they be directed on the path which leads to discipleship and sanctification in Christ.

My dearest Zachary, Elizabeth, and Daniel, may this book be a comfort to you as you follow Jesus.

# Contents

Foreword ..................................................... 11
Preface ...................................................... 13

### Part 1: The Call of Paul

The Fullness of God's Love ......................... 17
The Good Exchange .................................... 21
The Word Is Alive ....................................... 25
Divine Strength .......................................... 27
Peace in Grace ............................................ 29
Created, Called, Comforted ........................ 33
Believers and Disciples ............................... 37
Suffer for God ............................................ 41
Discipleship Imperative .............................. 43
A Life Well Lived ...................................... 49

### Part 2: Paul's Promises

The Message of Power ................................ 57
Your Test Results ....................................... 61
Glory and Joy ............................................. 63
Be Sanctified .............................................. 65
With Jesus Forever ..................................... 67
Sanctification Guarantee ............................. 69
Chosen to Be Saved .................................... 73
Life in Christ .............................................. 75

| | |
|---|---|
| Father | 77 |
| Faith through Love | 79 |
| Crucified | 81 |
| We Reap What We Sow | 85 |
| The Mind of Christ | 89 |
| One Way Out | 93 |
| For the Common Good | 95 |
| Baptized | 97 |
| God Is Love | 99 |
| Grace | 103 |
| Our Hope | 105 |
| Stand Firm | 109 |
| The Purpose of Comfort | 111 |
| Amen | 115 |
| Competence | 117 |
| The Glory of God | 119 |
| Live the Gospel | 121 |
| Life | 125 |
| Balance Due | 127 |
| Purpose | 129 |
| Purity | 133 |
| Brotherhood | 135 |
| Cheerful | 137 |
| Divine Power | 139 |
| Masquerade | 141 |
| Strength in Weakness | 145 |
| Authority in Weakness | 149 |
| Faith in the Gospel | 151 |
| Righteous Judgment | 155 |
| Righteousness by Faith | 159 |
| The Promise | 161 |

| | |
|---|---|
| Peace and Hope | 163 |
| All | 167 |
| Dead to Sin | 171 |
| Dead to the Law | 175 |
| Two Masters | 179 |
| Free in Christ | 183 |
| Help Is Here | 187 |
| God's Purpose | 191 |
| The Love of God | 195 |
| Who Are You? | 199 |
| Discipleship | 201 |
| To Know God's Will | 203 |
| Humble Service | 207 |
| God's Sovereignty | 211 |
| Love Is Everything | 213 |
| Every Knee | 215 |
| Clean and Unclean | 217 |
| Paul's Comfort | 223 |
| Saved to Serve | 227 |
| | |
| Closing Thoughts | 231 |
| Endnotes | 233 |

# Foreword

I have been a believer for fifty years. I have helped three Spirit-filled denominations grow in the Lord.

The Word of God is new every morning, no matter how long you have been a believer. The Word of the Lord does not get old, just better.

This book will be a wonderful reading for your daily quiet time and also for study in small groups. Travis has truly been led by the Holy Spirit, giving so much of himself for the benefit others.

There is nothing to compare with the power of the Holy Spirit. You would be missing out on a great deal not having read this book: *Paul's Comfort*. This book is for new and old in the Lord and for those looking for answers.

—Nicholson H. Griggs

# Preface

The extraordinary life is the one placed faithfully and fully into the will of God. The extraordinary life is lived by allowing Jesus Christ to live His life through you. The only means of living this life is by faith in the promises of God.

Christ lived so that we may live this extraordinary life of love. God loves the world—His creation—and every man, woman, and child He placed in it. Grace abounds to all by His pleasure and mercy.

Live a life worthy of the calling you have received: to love like Jesus. You have been saved to serve and are free in Christ to love! Submit your heart to God as an open cup ready to receive His Word and all the blessings that come with Him.

Apostle Paul lived possibly the most extraordinary life ever lived for the sake of the Gospel of Jesus Christ, and he lived it abounding in joy, peace, and love. His ministry was a reflection of Christ living inside of Him by the power of the Holy Spirit. His message was simple: Christ has set you free to live a life of love in service to God, who saved you with mercy and grace, not of works that any man should boast, but for good works, in order to advance His kingdom.

# Part 1
## The Call of Paul

# The Fullness of God's Love

God loves Satan.[1] Does that trouble you? To understand God's love, we must understand creation.

God is the only timeless One, and through Christ, all things were created and created by Him for Him. God is good, beautiful, perfect, loving, righteous, holy, merciful, and just. When Satan rebelled, God showed him the gracious mercy of His love as his Creator by exiling him from heaven.[2]

God could have destroyed him then. Instead, God allowed Satan to carry on for a time so that His love, mercy, and justice would be perfectly displayed before the heavenly powers and authorities, the angels, and eventually, before us. Only God knew that Jesus would die for the world to reconcile it to Himself and thereby defeat Satan with perfect justice.

Only when we are tenderly shown the consequences of our actions can the punishment be understood by ourselves to be just, even though it was just to the Judge from the onset. God never has and never will force His will on us, although He is a mighty persuader! All of our choices are of our own free agency, which was granted to us as a gift of grace so that we would choose Him freely. Love cannot be successfully forced on anyone; it has to be freely given and freely received to be God-love.

So as hard as it may be to accept, God loves Satan—not just loved, but still loves, even though he has already been judged and condemned for his actions. It is this same love that allows a mother to love her son as he spends life in prison for murdering his brother. If this kind of love is possible here in us, then it must have originated from our Creator and be representative of the love of God for every one He created, whether man, angel, or, yes, even Satan. So Satan is loved by God still, which day-by-day makes his judgment all the worse for himself.

So it is with us. God gave us free will as a gift so that we would freely love Him. He created us in His image so that He could lavish His love on us and commune with us.

God is all-knowing about the beginning and the end, for He created time and then placed creation inside of it. God knew we would rebel because of Satan's rebellion, but He made us anyway. God placed Adam in the garden and enjoyed him for a long and precious time before it all went wrong for Adam.

God began by protecting us from Satan and still does today. If it were Satan's choice alone, we all would be destroyed, but God protects us by His grace. He only allows us to be tempted with as much as we can handle and always provides a way out, until we fully reject Him—then honoring our freewill choice of rebellion, God gives us over to our sin since it is what we have proven to Him and the heavens that is our heart's desire.

God knew Adam would sin but created him anyway in love. God protected him in the garden and gave him only one simple law, and Adam could have simply chosen to say no, but with desires to please self and others before God, just like we do when we sin, Adam chose to obey Eve rather than God.

Simple rebellion, simple consequences, permanent result: death. Adam would have lived for eternity, communing with Eve and God in the garden, but because of his freewill choice, sin corrupted mankind and forever carried with it physical and emotional death following the spiritual death from sin. But like Satan's stay of execution, granted only by mercy and grace, mankind's stay of execution for sin carries on.

Our problem of course is not being good or bad, but being dead versus alive. We live with physical and soulful life here on earth, but our spiritual self, the self created to bear the image of God, is dead as a result of our actions and corruption from Adam.

Sin is defined as knowing what is right and not doing it.[3] What is right is placed inside the heart of a man's soul by the Creator. It is impossible for a human not to sin. No two-year-old ever made it to the age of three without a magnificent display of selfishness and disobedience: sin. Willful rebellion is the heart's nature: sin. It is unavoidable but curable: the remedy is Christ!

God loved us enough to bear our sinful flesh, resist all temptation, and die a criminal's death on a Roman cross as the innocent Lamb of God. Jesus to take upon Himself the sin-debt of every man, woman, and child from Adam to you so that we would not have to die as a result of sin.[4] That is how much God loves you.[5]

# The Good Exchange

The only way to be with God is to be cleansed from sin, because God is holy and, by default, cannot be in the presence of sin[6]—His glory would burn us up.[7]

God placed knowledge of Himself and His moral code within the heart of man.[8] He calls us all to repentance and beckons us to choose Him as a result of the love He has shown to us by creating us. He graciously does not call us to be good or bad until after we are regenerated. Until we are saved, He calls us to be spiritually alive rather than spiritually dead. God perfectly created life and circumstance for each one of us so that the measure of faith needed to affect salvation is necessarily provided.

In the Day of Judgment, we will all know that the unsaved freely chose death rather than life, however sad, because of God's perfect love and perfect justice. Grace then will become the expired reward for the unsaved; they will be sad but also satisfied that God created them, gave them the choice of life or death, and rewarded them accordingly out of His love, mercy, and grace.

Those that choose sin and disobedience have the reward they chose; if they desired to have God instead of the lusts of this world, they would have chosen Him. Their lives will be revealed like a scroll, and justice will be perfectly undeniable.[9]

We should all be justly destroyed at the end of our lives because of sin, but God desired to save man as an inheritance for His Son. You did nothing to be saved, but a lot to remain unsaved. God chose you like He chose Abraham, Moses, the prophets, and the apostles; He simply chose them.[10]

God loves this world now as He did when He created it. God loves us as He did when He created Adam. God made a way for us to be delivered from sin and live eternally again.[11] God freed us from bondage to this world, the law, and the penalty of death. Why? For His Son. As a gift to Jesus, we are His eternal bride. Why now? In order that we would show love to the world and all those in it that are perishing.

Jesus lived and ministered to the needy and called out unrighteousness and devils. We were saved not because of good works but for good works. Our purpose is to love like Jesus. If we cling to the pleasures of this world instead of following Jesus, we make our salvation of no value to God or the world we live in and are rebelling, yet again, like a selfish child.

Those that are perishing deserve God's love. They will see this love through us if we are sanctifying ourselves in the Word. We must love them with tender truth, sacrificial service, and unconditional compassion.

Jesus poured His lifeblood out into the ground of this earth for everyone, not just those He saved.[12] Accept it. This means that you are no more loved by God then the blatant and unrepentant sinner who dies in his transgressions, denying his Creator. So if God loves them and lived on earth to show His love for them, then saved us so He could continue to live His life through us,[13] what are we to do?

Jesus commands us now.[14] We are no longer free to do what we will, for we were bought with a price and the highest price ever paid in eternity for anything or anyone: the blood of the eternal living God.[15] You are no longer free to do as you choose but are commanded to live a life of love. You must love God and love fellow man. This is your purpose for being saved; this is your command from your King!

We have been freed from this world and made new vessels for the Spirit of God who gives us spiritual life. All this in order that we would allow Jesus to live through us and glorify the Father for the gracious gift of His magnificent love.

We must make ourselves slaves to Christ now and die to ourselves.[16] This is only possible through the indwelling presence of the Holy Spirit. He shows us how to live like Jesus, and we must learn to listen to Him and obey Him.[17]

Most of us spent many years living for ourselves and following after the world, so we cannot expect to live like Jesus as soon as we are saved. But we are now bent toward His will instead of our own. We must die to our own will a little more each day by putting our faith in the promises of His Word.

# The Word Is Alive

The living Word of God is the Bible as we have it today. It is inerrant, historically accurate, and spiritually alive.[18] Believe it. Until you accept by faith that the Bible is all true, you will not be able to live an extraordinary life. You cannot put your faith in a promise if you cannot faithfully accept that the promise was spoken by the living God.

If you do not have faith that the Bible is the perfect and inerrant Word of God, the best you can do is put your faith in the men who wrote it and have been dead for thousands of years. If you can't believe that Jesus commanded you to sell everything and give it to the poor and follow Him,[19] then how can you say that believing in Him has given you eternal life? You must have faith in something.

Where is your faith? Is it in good works or in the work of Christ on the cross?[20] If we say we trust in Jesus but deny that He has instructed us to live a life of sacrificial love, spread the Gospel, and make disciples, we deceive ourselves, and the truth is not in us.[21]

You must believe in everything the Bible says is true about Jesus Christ in order to qualify as a true believer.[22] You must believe the Bible is true about everything; otherwise, you have no basis for accepting that what it says about Jesus can be true. It is supernatural and extraordinary that Jesus was raised from the dead and especially that by believing it will affect in you a new heart and eternal life by God's grace.[23]

So if you believe that a supernatural God raised Jesus from the dead to save you, then you absolutely must accept that He can write a book, and write it accurately and exactly as He desires, so as to be able to breathe His life into it. The Word is alive and can be alive in you if you believe it and accept by faith that it is true for you.

# Divine Strength

Before we can look at the promises of God poured into the life of Paul, we must have already established that the Holy Bible is perfect and true, and I hope we have. Next we must understand that Jesus lived so that we would first be saved, know what is expected of us, then know the supernatural power promised to us to fulfill the purpose for our life.[24]

Hopefully you have already read the first book in this series: *The Gospel Message*. If not, I recommend you read it now and place your complete faith in those promises from Jesus first, accepting that God saved you for a purpose.

As we look at the life of Paul and the promises of God in his Epistles, we will do so with the presupposition and hope that you, the reader, have already agreed to follow Jesus and placed your life in His will. And you also understand that God has given you access to everything you could possibly need,[25] with unending blessings and rewards, for simply obeying His command to love.

Paul was called to follow Jesus, be a witness of the Gospel, and make disciples. He was called and sanctified so that the life Jesus wants us to live can be seen reflected in the life of Paul.

We can argue that we can't have faith like the apostles because we did not walk with Jesus. We can argue that performing works of love and miracles like Jesus did is not possible since we are sinners. But excuses are, of course, not relevant, as Jesus promised we would be empowered to do even greater works through the gift of the Holy Spirit.[26]

We cannot deny the life of Paul. He was the worst of men: a Christian killer; self-appointed to persecute the early church. He was, despite how sinful, chosen by God to be saved and called to serve Jesus in love to mankind. It is the same with us. We are saved and called to serve mankind in love.[27]

Paul lived an extraordinary life serving Christ, and he did so by the power of Christ living inside of him.[28] Not only did Paul survive his mission, defy his own persecutors, and complete his race, but he did so with great joy and peace. How? Through the Comforter.

Paul's comfort was faith in the promises of God. The Holy Spirit spoke directly to Paul so that there was absolutely no question if he heard from God, and no doubt that he should put the promise to the test for God's great glory.

The Holy Spirit comforted Paul along his journey of sacrificially following Jesus through eternal promises. God is faithful and true, and He has protected those precious promises that were good enough for Paul, within His living Word.

## Peace in Grace

Peace can only be found in God.[29] Grace is sufficient for us at all times.[30] The gift of peace is essential to the Gospel, for by Christ's atonement, we are reconciled to the Father. We have peace because God no longer sees us as sinners but as children. The cross now stands between us and God, and God only sees us through His perfect love displayed on the cross. The cross is a sin-filter by which God views us.[31]

It is good that days are so short when we slip; God's mercies are new every morning.[32] Today is the day of salvation.[33] Did I think that I was immune to this? How easy it is to slip—one glance, one thought, one word—and the temptation door is open to sin.

We must spend each day with the Lord and feed our spirit before feeding our flesh. The armor of God must be put on like mail before we clothe ourselves with outer coverings.[34] Each day, the flesh pulls against the spirit, and what we feed grows stronger.[35] If we awake and feed the flesh yet neglect the feeding of our spirit, our flesh is positioned in strength to get its way if left unchecked.[36]

My peace is in the grace of God.[37] The Gospel is my comfort,[38] and the Holy Spirit within me is my Comforter.[39] My flesh is burdened with guilt, regret, shame, sorrow, pain, and disappointment. But these are cancers of the fall, and the devil fans the flames. The Holy Spirit comforts me in that all of these are covered by the blood of Christ so that I am free from tension, negativity, and all manner of unfaithfulness and sin.[40] I am only to look at the cross, and I see God looking back at me in perfect love. He immediately says to me, "The past is the past, whether yesterday, yesteryear, or thirty seconds ago. Come. We will continue on in love unto the day of perfection when no more tears will be shed.[41] I love you and see only hope and joy in your tomorrow. My grace has set you free."

My comfort is made real to me when I determine to accept that there is nothing I can do to cause God to love me less, and even so, nothing I can do to have God accept me more.[42] I am compelled to get back up and praise the God of mercy![43] I am even forced to do good things because He does good to me.

There is no condemnation for me,[44] for I have been permanently baptized into the living body of Christ, the perfect, holy, and glorified Body.[45] I am not judged when I sin; Satan is already judged, and I am already justified.[46] I am not a disappointment to Him when I fail to fulfill His perfect will and do good works. I am already sanctified;[47] I am perfect in Christ.[48]

My peace is therefore made perfect in the grace of God. If grace is an ocean, I am a boat going up and down, but only because I watch the waves; God sees me from above where I only appear to move forward to Christ.

In my valleys, it is only grace. On my mountains, it

is only grace. My heart beats each second because of grace. I turn from my sin and repent because of the Holy Spirit convicting me. I do good in the eyes of God by grace. I can only respond to the will of God. I cannot sway God to accept my works as good, only carry out the tasks He has chosen as effecting good. There is nothing I can do to change God's love and desire for me. His promises are eternal, and they comfort me each day.

# Created, Called, Comforted

Why did Jesus choose Saul of Tarsus to be the greatest apostle and write two-thirds of the New Testament? Was Saul so dangerous to the early church that God had to either convert him or eliminate him? Why didn't Jesus choose one of the original twelve apostles to take the Gospel to the Gentiles?

Jesus chose Saul as a perfect example to us all of what Christ can do to change a man. Even the worst Christian-murdering sinner was no match for the power of God's plan of salvation. Saul is our proof that God saves a man and for absolutely no reason of our own ability, worth, or merit.

In the eyes of a holy God, we were all Sauls deserving death before He chose us and made us Pauls by grace. There is no different type of salvation experience for anyone who has accepted Christ and become a child of God. Like Saul, you were once blind but now see; it is grace alone that saved you.[49] You did not talk God into saving you by being "good," for being "good" or "not good" was never the issue; you were dead, but now you live![50]

Christ chose Saul to show us what a life of faith in the power of the Gospel looks like. The apostles all walked with Jesus; it was easy for them to believe, especially once the Holy Spirit came to them. But Saul was called, however abruptly and powerfully, to believe by faith.

God measures out the faith we need to believe, and Saul was so far to the left of faith-center that it took a full-blown sight and sound vision to believe, with physical ailment! God did not leave Saul without comfort, however. Saul was baptized into the body of Christ and given the Holy Spirit, same as we were the instant we were saved.[51]

Saul was chosen to be Paul by the Father as an inheritance to His Son and as a worker for Christ's kingdom. Of whom much is given, much is required. Thus, Paul joyfully spent the rest of his life sacrificially proclaiming the Gospel message he received.

Jesus gave us the life of Paul so that we could all seek to emulate his life. Our lives as sinners saved by grace are to be like Paul's. He did not sell all his possessions and give them to the poor; instead, he became poor, meek in spirit, and humble to the cross so that the richness of the Gospel might pour out of him like it did from his precious Lord.[52]

To live on this earth as a believer means to be Christ, and to die is gain: eternal life, blessings, and rewards. Jesus ended His days on earth with the commands to love,[53] spread the Gospel,[54] and make disciples.[55] As the risen King of glory, Jesus did the saving of Paul, same as He has saved us all.

Paul obeyed Jesus and wrote the letters of the New Testament so we too could be comforted with the comfort Paul was comforted with.[56] Having the promises of God in the complete Holy Bible, it should be easy for us to be comforted while we do good works and live out our salvation.

Paul learned the promises by experience and direct inspiration from the Holy Spirit. We now have the living written Word and all the promises of God needed to faithfully live the extraordinary life. Paul truly and fully lived out the life that Jesus commissioned before He left.

Paul lived so that we could read his story and have confidence in God's provision while we selflessly seek His will and magnificently display the work of God in us. Our purpose is to live a life of service to the will of God—to spread His great news and do works of love and mercy. You are appointed a time here in this place.[57] Make it worthwhile, for who of you can add a single hour to your life?[58]

If you are seeking comfort in the things of this world, you are losing rewards and blessings by the day.[59] If you accept by faith that God created you and sustains your life by grace, then you will know that every heartbeat is counted, just like every hair is known, and every thought about you is measured.[60]

Paul's life is to encourage us to place our faith in the promises of God to achieve supernatural results for the cause of Christ. The faithfulness of God to Paul shall comfort us as we do His work. God gave us promises in action in the life of Paul. As we step out in faith to do good works, we do so with holy comfort and assurance.

# Believers and Disciples

We are all called to be Pauls. Christ lived so that we would know how a child of God is to live, doing good and showing love to God's glory. Paul lived to prove that the Christian life is not only possible but assured, because of the gift of the Holy Spirit and Christ living inside of us.

We are all called to live like Paul, taking the Gospel to the world: one man, one woman, one child at a time; one nation, one town, one place at a time.

Paul was given the Holy Spirit to comfort him with new promises of God's faith as we set out on a mission to fulfill his purpose for salvation. God, through Paul, has given us these same promises to comfort us as we purpose to do the same: follow Jesus. And we have the same Spirit to give us joy and peace in God's faithfulness to those promises.

God did not save us just to live an assured life of salvation when we die. He saved us to live an assured life of salvation here and now! We already have eternal life, so why should we care about the things of this world?[61] Surely God will bless us more abundantly in the new heaven and new earth forever.[62]

We are to follow Jesus. He saved us so we would follow Him.[63] The problem with this world is not that there aren't enough Christians. No, the problem is that too many Christians are not following Jesus!

If we would wake up to the purpose of our salvation, this world would be a different place; there would not be so many consequences for so many disobedient children, and this nation would be safer, more godly, more merciful, and even more gracious with its wealth toward the suffering and hopeless.

Change starts with us. We are to strive to change one life at a time with the good news. We are to change one life at a time with the sacrificial love of Christ in us. We are to change one life at a time and disciple a brother or sister in Christ needing a resurrection from the trials and desires of self.

Paul's conversion was intense.[64] He was filled with the Holy Spirit three days later and immediately began to proclaim to the world a message which he could not keep to himself.[65] For Paul, it took only three days from his salvation until he was filled with the Holy Spirit and made a follower of Jesus. Paul owes his awakening to the purpose of his life to an obedient follower of Jesus named Ananias. We are to understand that to disciple the way Ananias and the others discipled Saul still holds true today: we are to disciple out of obedience to our Lord. If a man is saved and never discipled, he can spend years, and even his whole life in the same "Woe is me" condition that lasted but three days for Saul.

Jesus could have filled Saul with the Holy Spirit Himself. But instead, He wanted us to understand the difference between salvation and discipleship. Getting saved is an act of Jesus; being a disciple is an act of man's obedience. A disciple is an obedient Christian and, by nature, makes other disciples. We must disciple each other. This is Jesus's command to us all as it was to Ananias for Saul so that we would be awakened to the purpose of our salvation and be filled with the Holy Spirit to do the will of God for our lives.

> For three days he was blind, and did not eat or drink anything. (Acts 9:9, NIV)

For Saul, it was only three days that he was blind to his purpose for salvation. We must work to show new converts the purpose of their salvation! If we settle for "we got them saved," we tragically deceive ourselves, for only Jesus saves, and they would have been saved along the way anyway, for those given to Jesus by the Father (not by us) will in no way go unsaved.[66]

Leading someone to Christ and then leaving them in the crib unclothed, underfed, and ignored is terrible. We might as well have left them unsaved so the devil would not have been made aware of their predestined salvation.[67]

It is imperative that we disciple new believers, else we are just selfish siblings. We must obey Jesus to spread the Gospel and then make disciples of those who believe. Would you give birth to a new baby and then leave her in a garbage can? Sadly, there are infant abandonment horror stories, let alone the epic tragedy of abortion, to compare this to. Please do get the picture and the seriousness of the matter.

When we are saved, we are as infants in Christ and cannot fend for ourselves in the spirit world.[68] The spirit world all around us is more real than the world we see with our natural eyes. We cannot let new believers fend for themselves. The devil has had almost two thousand years to perfect his attack on new believers: mere infants in Christ.

The devil cannot keep Christ from saving those the Father has predestined to be adopted to sonship, but the devil is an expert at keeping new believers from following Jesus. Infants in Christ are no threat to Satan's kingdom, but disciples are! If we lead someone to Christ and do not see to it that they are discipled (clothed and fed with the living Word), we indirectly make their salvation of no use and leave them to the dogs.

Picture Saul blind, starving, and thirsty for three days, and you get a perfect picture of a new believer from the moment of his salvation until someone shows him the will of God for their life and the power of the Word in them. As Paul was blind, hungry, and thirsty, so an un-discipled new believer is blind to the purpose for their salvation, starved of the Word of God, and thirsty for the water of life.

# Suffer for God

We are all enemies of God until God intervenes and draws us to Him and turns our hearts of stone into hearts of flesh where He can take up His residence.[69] God saves us to serve.[70]

Jesus saved us from the penalty of our sin but not necessarily the consequences of our sin. Paul was terrible before his conversion, killing and approving of killing Christians.[71] Terrible! And the persecution goes on yet today.[72] Yet how many people did we kill with hate, resentment, jealousy, anger, selfishness, deceit, or rejection through the years?[73] Jesus said that to God, even these are as murders committed in our heart.

If given a writ of authority from the government as "God's leaders and defenders," would we not have acted as Paul, zealous for God and the Law, or even as the Jewish mobs that tried to kill Jesus?[74] Don't think so highly of yourself. Sin left unchecked by the grace of God led to Cain killing his brother and the "chosen of God" killing the Messiah on a Roman cross.

> But the Lord said to Ananias, "Go! This man is my chosen instrument to proclaim my name to the Gentiles and their kings and to the people of Israel. I will show him how much he must suffer for my name." (Acts 9:15–16, NIV)

So Paul was selected by Christ as His "chosen instrument" to serve Him. The consequences for a life of sin will ultimately bear their fruit even once saved. However Jesus would show Paul how much he would suffer for Jesus's name's sake. Yet this is the beginning of Paul's comfort. Paul would find it all joy to suffer for Jesus, for Jesus suffered for him and died a criminal's death to save us all from our murderous hearts.

We have a choice when we are saved, one we did not have before. We can choose to follow self and suffer for our sins for no benefit to ourselves, the church, or God, or we can choose to follow Jesus and suffer for His kingdom. We will suffer the consequences of our life of sin nonetheless; we might as well be blessed by the Lord in the midst of our suffering by serving Him.

# Discipleship Imperative

Ananias obediently ministered to the new convert named Saul, and by doing such, Saul regained his sight and strength through the filling of the Holy Spirit.

> Then Ananias went to the house and entered it. Placing his hands on Saul, he said, "Brother Saul, the Lord—Jesus, who appeared to you on the road as you were coming here—has sent me so that you may see again and be filled with the Holy Spirit." Immediately, something like scales fell from Saul's eyes, and he could see again. He got up and was baptized, and after taking some food, he regained his strength. (Acts 9:17–19, NIV)

Paul was saved on the road to Damascus and indwelt by the Holy Spirit, forever changed and reconciled unto God. But it was not until another follower of Jesus ministered unto Saul's newly reborn spirit that he would see the truth. Through the laying on of hands, Paul was filled with the power of the Holy Spirit needed to live the Christian life and testify to the name of Jesus. After this, Paul was formally baptized, but after he had already been baptized into the Body of Christ by the Word of God on the road to Damascus, and after he was filled by the Holy Spirit through the hands of Ananias. This public baptism is an act of obedience and seals our hearts in the presence of men and angels as faithful followers of the will of Jesus Christ.[75]

After this rather efficient salvation, filling, consecration, and baptismal process for Saul, he was immediately discipled by the believers in Damascus. Ananias and the others, even though Saul was a Christian-killer, were obedient to Jesus's command to disciple Saul.

The impact of quickly feeding Saul with the Word of God was his effective preaching of the very same Gospel message almost at once. His calling to take the Gospel to the Gentiles was being realized with full power almost immediately!

The process of Saul's conversion is detailed for us so that we would understand the importance to disciple new believers. If we minister to them quickly, their ministry will quickly be seen, for Christ saved us all so that we would serve Him now, not serve ourselves for a time and hope to later serve Him.

We are saved to serve and ready to serve as soon as we are fed and discipled by other disciples. It is everyone's responsibility to disciple new believers.[76] It is God's responsibility to convict and comfort them through the Holy Spirit and make the Word of God effective inside of them.[77] If we do not feed these early believers with the Word, the devil will come to feed them with doubt, lies, shame, guilt, and the lusts of this world.[78]

Saul's conversion experience is the same for all believers. Jesus saves. The Holy Spirit seals. Jesus compels the church: "Minister to the new convert." Christ is ready to intercede with the promise of the Holy Spirit to fill them with power to serve the Father. However this power can only be given once the babe in Christ is taught how to properly handle it.

The believer is baptized in obedience by water or oil through the laying on of hands of a disciple. The believer is taught about Jesus Christ and the way by a faithful disciple's words. Notice that God's responsibility ends at the salvation part. The Holy Spirit convicts but does not feed. It is the church's responsibility to make sure the discipleship process begins and is sustained. It is the believer's responsibility to be fed with the Word of God and to put into practice what he has learned. The Holy Spirit then makes that applied Word come to pass, and God is shown faithful to His promises.[79]

This is how we live extraordinary lives. It all starts with a disciple obediently ministering to a new believer so that after the accept Jesus they are not left to the vultures blind, hungry, and thirsty on the side of the road. It is the church's responsibility to disciple new believers, not God's responsibility, and not the pastor's responsibility.

Do we want the world saved, or do we want to save the world? Do we want Christ to live in them, or do we selfishly hide Him to ourselves? The church that leads men to Christ to number count, then lets those new believers fend for themselves is disobedient to the command of Christ. A well-running machine will pair up a new believer with a faithful follower to make sure they are sanctified so that Jesus would gain a skilled new worker for His kingdom.

This is what is at stake. Yes, it is work, and it takes time, but if we turn our backs on new believers, we are turning our backs on Jesus and His commands. Jesus told us to feed His sheep, not find them. Jesus finds them then gives them to us to feed. We are the voice, but the Holy Spirit gives the ear that hears.[80]

It is not the pastor's job to feed His sheep; it is the church's job. What if the disciples in Damascus would have disobeyed Jesus and turned their backs on Saul the way we turn our backs on new believers as a congregation, Sunday after Sunday? We may not have two-thirds of the New Testament! What are we missing now that could be different if only we would have discipled our brothers and sisters and taught them the purpose of their salvation?

The problem in this world is not that there aren't enough Christians. The problem is that the church is failing to disciple them. We are left with full churches on Sunday of Christians who think tithing is the greatest service they have been called to do, and they still can't do it! We are left with disillusioned pastors who feel they are beating the wind. We are left with unfulfilled lives and troubled souls, and we ask ourselves why? We see churches filled with people but not with the Holy Spirit. We see churches filled with people searching to be fed but starved by the world and the ruler of it.

The promises of God are not written on our heart when we are saved; the presence of God is. The promises of God are written on our heart through study in the Word of God. A new believer, however, rarely starts reading the Bible with a passion for years after their salvation, unless someone leads them through it and teaches them how to eat spiritual food.

Discipleship begins with spoon-feeding an infant in Christ. Any mother will tell you that raising an infant is hard but rewarding work, confident that they were called to the task. Let us all seek to find an infant in Christ to feed. We all have something to offer if we are saved. It is most likely that you will both grow together and receive solid food from one another and become more mature followers of the Lord in unity.

Paul's comfort was in God's faithfulness to His promises.[81] These promises were written on his heart as Paul sought the face of God. The written Word had not yet been created, so it came to Paul through the spoken Word from the disciples and the inspired Word by the Holy Spirit. We have the written Word but must again start with the spoken Word to create a palette for the written Word to be inscribed on a young believer's heart.

We are comforted as God makes His promises come to pass for us when we follow Jesus in service. First, these promises must be written on our heart through the study of the Word, but even before that, the church must spoon-feed the new believer so that he may taste that the Lord is good and learn how to walk in the Spirit with baby steps.[82]

The church is responsible for raising spiritual children to mature and serve Christ. However, it seems like we are only interested in saving people and then making them feel guilty if they are not putting their tithe in the bucket every Sunday. Then we wonder why the church struggles and is left without comfort and joy.

Paul had comfort and joy because he was discipled immediately after he was saved. The Word was well planted in his heart when he was hungry, and it grew to produce amazing and supernatural fruit.

While we explore Paul's comfort in this study, let us be continually reminded where this comfort originated. The Word of God was fed to Saul in Damascus by obedient and faithful followers of Jesus.

We are disciples of Christ if we follow and obey. We follow and obey by loving those in the world. We love those in the world if we are spreading the Gospel and teaching new believers about Jesus and His precious promises.

Can you say you are a follower of Jesus? Are you a faithful disciple? If you are being comforted by the Word of God and display the fruit of the Spirit in your life, then you are realizing the peace of God.[83] The Holy Spirit comforts us through the promises of God and His faithfulness. Paul's comfort is to be our comfort as we seek to follow and serve Jesus.

# A Life Well Lived

Great mention is made of Paul's three missionary journeys, but that is only because Luke groups them into three general time frames in Acts. Paul had at least six distinct missionary journeys.

Paul's first mission consisted of the years after his conversion and discipleship in Damascus and his preaching to the Gentiles in Tarsus and the surrounding regions until Barnabas brought him to minister in Antioch. Then the three broader travel periods Luke details in Acts ensued.

Paul's fifth missionary journey was his lengthy trip to Rome. Paul preached the Gospel in many cities and strengthened the brethren along the way. He then continued on with the same good works while in Rome for two more years.

We know little about his ministry after his release from Roman imprisonment, or honorable detainment until his trial as it may be called, except for references from early church fathers and non-canonical epistles. However Paul definitely went on a major mission trip after his release from Rome, and this is his sixth journey. Good evidence suggests that Paul went to Spain during this time,[84] and many support that Paul even made it to the British Isles before he was arrested and taken to Rome for his final imprisonment and execution.[85]

## Paul's Comfort

We are confident from Paul's final three Epistles that he wrote 1 Timothy and Titus during his sixth missionary journey and 2 Timothy during his second imprisonment before his execution. Paul's tone in Ephesians, Colossians, Philippians, and Philemon, said to have been written during his first imprisonment, is much more confident than in the 2 Timothy letter. Paul was confident during his first imprisonment, for the Lord told him he would go to Rome and witness there.[86] Paul's comfort by the Holy Spirit dictates that. His strength was from the Lord Himself living in him.

As Christ agonized in the garden before His death, so did Paul agonize in Rome during his second imprisonment before his death. Knowing that Paul was so personified by the life of Christ gives us little doubt as to the ministries he conducted, mission trips he made, and true circumstances he was in, through the tone, emotion, and passion of his letters.

Paul realized Christ living inside of him to the fullest possible extent. James Stalker says of this:

> Indeed, so perfectly was Christ formed in him that we can now study Christ's character in his, and beginners may perhaps learn even more of Christ from studying Paul's life than from studying Christ's own.[87]

The words, anguish, joy, peace, frustration, anger, love, and sacrifice of Paul are no doubt to us those of the Savior. We must take what Paul writes as if Jesus Himself speaks the words directly to us. Christ gave Paul His words, emotions, love, and all of His other characteristics and attributes, including powers, miracles, and healings, that Jesus Himself possessed as the Son of man, and now possesses with authority to pour out onto His disciples by His good will, as the risen and glorified Lord.

God's desire is that we know Him, love Him, and serve Him. But mankind's condition had grown so completely unable to hear the truth that Jesus had to leave so that the Holy Spirit could come. It is the Spirit who now speaks directly into our transformed hearts, bypassing our sinful flesh, blinded minds, and troubled souls. James Stalker again says of this:

> But it was one of the most pathetic aspects of his earthly ministry that he could not tell all his mind to his followers. They were not able to bear it; they were too rude and limited to take it in. He had to carry his deepest thoughts out of the world with him unuttered, trusting with a sublime faith that the Holy Ghost would lead his Church to grasp them in the course of its subsequent development. Even what he did utter was very imperfectly understood.[88]

So the life Paul led was indeed the life Christ wanted to lead and chose to lead through him in order to effectively reach the hearts of men and demonstrate to them God's love and power. The words of Christ, spoken to our hearts through the indwelling presence of His Holy Spirit, were Paul's comfort. No one can deny what they know in their heart to be true. The life of abandon for Christ speaks louder than any words. Love is the universal language. Love never fails.[89]

Paul did not merely take three missionary journeys,

or even six. Paul's life from the time of his salvation until his death was one, single, nonstop missionary journey. He only paused for a while in certain locations to strengthen the believers there and make disciples, be strengthened himself by the church, and of course, write the letters, which are now known as his canonical epistles.

We are all to be Pauls, for Paul lived as Christ desired him to live, with Christ living through him to His good purpose.[90] Paul died to himself and gave his life over to Christ.[91] His reward is the life of every Christian that ever came to know eternal salvation through his missions and letters. His rewards are probably the greatest in heaven of all the saints. And all because he followed Jesus and answered the calling on his heart.

Paul did not begin writing the canonical epistles until about fourteen years after his conversion, but his ministry was in full force within the first days of his salvation.[92, 93]

We will look at the promises of God given to Paul through a chronological study of his thirteen epistles. The understanding of the promises given to us as a result of the eternal ramifications of Jesus's death and resurrection were increasingly more powerfully understood and conveyed as he matured in his walk of faith.[94]

The order of this study is based on the order in which Paul likely wrote his letters, using many references and putting an order together that most could agree with, or at least not find it profitable to argue against.[95] As you reference for yourself the times and places of Paul's life, journeys, and writings, and you'll see that there is much debate to when and where Paul wrote the epistles, but of little importance to the end result of proclaiming the Gospel for the ages to come.

Again, the chronological order of this study is to develop a new and increasing awareness of the power of the maturing Word in you, made possible through Christ in you, made possible by the cross. This Word, maturing in the heart of Paul, was Paul's comfort. He was constantly fed promises and assurances by Christ through the Holy Spirit, in order that by faith, he would lead an extraordinary life changing the world into a place of love and hope.

Our Lord Jesus Christ desires that you also mature in the Word just the same, have fully convicted faith in His promises, and powerfully fulfill the purpose of your salvation: to change the world through love.

# Part 2
## Paul's Promises

# The Message of Power

> For we know, brothers and sisters loved by God, that he has chosen you, because our gospel came to you not simply with words but also with power, with the Holy Spirit and deep conviction. You know how we lived among you for your sake. You became imitators of us and of the Lord, for you welcomed the message in the midst of severe suffering with the joy given by the Holy Spirit.
>
> —1 Thessalonians 1:4–6 (NIV)

To know a believer is to know the transformational power of the cross. Any believer has had his or her own heart of stone magnificently turned into a heart of flesh so that the Holy Spirit would find a clean residence. This transformation is instantaneous. God chooses the sinner, transforms the heart in an instant, and breathes His Spirit in to permanently reside.[96] The sinner is now saved eternally, for their spirit is made alive by the presence of God.[97]

In the spiritual world, the power displayed by this change must shake the heavens.[98] The believer knows he or she has been changed, and the sinner begins to display a shift in personality and direction, being convicted to do good instead of evil, and convicted to repent instead of feeding self-desire.[99] There is no positioning a man can make to prepare for this radical death-to-life change. God chooses the heart and does all this restorative resurrection work Himself.[100]

A man can believe God exists, believe that He can save, and do good deeds in the sight of man, but without the display of the power of transformation, instantaneous and progressive, there is no salvation.

There is a way to know if a man is saved or not. It may take time to draw it out of a fallen saint, but every child of God has a story to tell: of a time when their heart was changed; of a moment when they felt the power and conviction to follow Christ.[101]

Free will only starts once a man is saved. Before then, he was dead and could only serve himself. Upon salvation, the Holy Spirit frees him from the penalty of sin, and the course of true life begins.

Did you quench the power, or feed your newborn spirit?[102] Are you a day closer to your holy marriage, or did you lose sight of your first love?[103] The power is still within you. Repent and feed your spirit with the Word of God, call for the conviction that came with your calling, and cry out to Jesus. His love has never left you. May the power cell already placed within you give you peace.

*God's Promise:*

There is only one Gospel message, and upon those chosen to receive it, it comes with the power of the Holy Spirit.

# Your Test Results

> On the contrary, we speak as those approved
> by God to be entrusted with the gospel.
> We are not trying to please people but God,
> who tests our hearts.
>
> —1 Thessalonians 2:4 (NIV)

The message of hope has been entrusted to every child of God. His life, death, and resurrection belong to you. Jesus has promised even to live His holy and perfect life through you in order to love the world.[104]

What have you done with the message of salvation? Have you hid it inside of your heart for fear of the world's judgment? Fear God's perfect judgment instead for how you thanked Him for saving you and investing the blood of His Son in you.

God knows your heart's intent because He lives in you. Every thought goes on before Him like a banner and is written down. Every thought will be tested, and you will be accountable for them on Judgment Day.[105]

The unsaved are already judged, and their reward is death and eternal separation from God.[106] Their preparation, if to be saved, is by holy whispers and the pull of the loving message of hope spoken through the lives and mouths of believers.[107]

We have our hearts measured, monitored, and weighed by the perfect and just Lord who loves us and desires that we become like Him.[108] It is not a test with a secret score revealed after grading; it is a test that comes with the thought by thought, deed by deed conviction of the living Spirit inside of you. We can ignore the test results but cannot deny them.

The fear of the Lord is to hate that which is evil.[109] Weigh every thought and action against the cross. Seek to honor the One who gave His life for you. Ask the Teacher every day, if not by every thought and deed, what the score was on the test, and He will hold, love, and direct your paths to a life of success, blessing, and peace.[110]

*God's Promise:*
God knows the root of every thought and deed and will bring perfect justice for each and every one.

# Glory and Joy

> For what is our hope, our joy, or the crown in which we will glory in the presence of our Lord Jesus when he comes? Is it not you? Indeed, you are our glory and joy.
>
> —1 Thessalonians 2:19–20 (NIV)

What is it that you look forward to on the day you meet Jesus? Your day could be today. What is your hope? Eternity started for you the day you were saved, so how you are spending it now on earth is a good sign of how you will spend it in heaven!

The kingdom of God was ushered in on Pentecost when the Holy Spirit began to take up residence in the hearts of men and begin the sanctification of Christ's bride.[111] We long for the crown of glory,[112] even many crowns, but how do we earn them?

We surely obtain the crown of life, but what about the crowns of love, righteousness, peace, compassion, sacrifice, and salvation?[113] Our hope of glory, fully revealed in the joyful face of Jesus on that great Day, is reserved for us in the lives of our dear brothers and sisters in the Lord. We shall celebrate with Jesus the lives our good labor of love has changed.

The Spirit testifies to this in us. It is seemingly inexplicable why I should take joy in giving my time and money away for no apparent earthly reward.[114] Our hope is in the joy of the Lord, and a simple glimpse of this joy is felt in our heart as we do more and more for the sake of the Gospel.

*God's Promise:*
The work of God is to save men through His Word living in and through you, for your future glory and eternal joy.

# Be Sanctified

> It is God's will that you should be sanctified.
> For God did not call us to be impure,
> but to live a holy life.
> Therefore, anyone who rejects this instruction
> does not reject a human being but God, the
> very God who gives you his Holy Spirit.
> —1 Thessalonians 4:3a,7–8 (NIV)

Our command is to be obedient children of our Father.[115] This is no different than the necessary relationship between a responsible parent and his or her child. We know what is good for them and only ask them to listen to us in order that they learn how to properly conduct themselves in relationship to others and the parents who love them so dearly.

Our Father commands us to be sanctified, to be separated from the ways of the world, and to live a holy life the way Jesus would live.[116] In order to discern God's will for our lives, we must obey what we already know to be true and commit our lives to being holy.

God has given us His Spirit to live in us so that this can be possible. He does not expect us to be perfect, but instead expects us to yearn for perfection and hate sin.[117]

The Holy Spirit comforts us on our path to be like Jesus and never condemns us.[118] If we disregard our command to be holy, we reject God Himself, for we have set ourselves on the side of our flesh and against the very presence of God living inside of us—even God the Holy Spirit.

The Holy Spirit was given to us in order that sanctification would be possible—even guaranteed! It is our inner man that is being transformed daily. We must feed our spirit with the Word of God in order to procure ever-increasing alignment with His will.[119]

As long as we accept the command to increase in holiness, He will make sure we succeed. With each failure we gain more knowledge, assurance, and faith in the God who loves us, encourages us, and will never leave or forsake us. The Holy Spirit is our Encourager, and He builds in us strong, undefeatable spirits.

*God's Promise:*
We cannot make ourselves holy, but God can and will, if we simply surrender to His purpose and grace.

# With Jesus Forever

> For the Lord himself will come down from heaven, with a loud command, with the voice of the archangel and with the trumpet call of God, and the dead in Christ will rise first. After that, we who are still alive and are left will be caught up together with them in the clouds to meet the Lord in the air. And so we will be with the Lord forever. Therefore encourage one another with these words.
>
> —1 Thessalonians 4:16–18 (NIV)

Paul knew deep within his heart and spirit that to die is to be united with Jesus forever. Jesus revealed to Him how glorious it will be when He returns for us. A trumpet blast will call forth the dust of the dead in Christ, and those who are alive will witness the resurrection of the dead many times over!

Paul was certainly encouraged with this vision each day he stretched forth his hand in service to Jesus. We must seek to be daily encouraged by the Second Coming, for this is Paul's instruction to us.

Are you excited to see Jesus on resurrection day? If so, you should be hastening that day with service to

Jesus, even to the point of death if that is God's will. Or are you worried about that day? A faithful believer should have no concerns and be able to say, "Father, I have sought Your will, followed Jesus, and loved like Him. I have finished the race well and deserve to be with You forever, for Christ Himself lives in me!"

Let the Second Coming of Christ always be on your mind. It could be today! Today you could die and see Jesus in a blink; today you may just hear the trumpet sound!

Will you be pleased to hear the trumpet sound today? Whatever you are doing, consider it in light of the trumpet sounding as the last thing you ever did on this earth. The time is too short to live to please yourself. Be always pleasing the Lord and encouraged by the joy of the Holy Spirit within you, beaming with excitement at the coming return of Jesus when He shall claim His bride.

*God's Promise:*
The believer will soon see Jesus, in the blink of an eye, and behold His glory.

# Sanctification Guarantee

> Do not quench the Spirit. May God himself,
> the God of peace, sanctify you through and
> through. May your whole spirit, soul and body
> be kept blameless at the coming of our Lord
> Jesus Christ. The one who calls you is
> faithful, and he will do it.
>
> —1 Thessalonians 5:19, 23–24 (NIV)

Paul knew the importance of cooperating with God. He knew firsthand that it was hard to kick against the pricks.[120] You have been called to be sanctified, but it is a process of cooperation. You must do your part, and God will do the rest. Sanctification is however guaranteed, one way or another, now, or later on that great Day. This is a promise!

God has invested the precious life and blood of His Son into you, and it is your fair duty to be therefore obedient, thankful, and blameless. Remain in His Word, for it defeats temptation through the strengthening of your spirit.

The Holy Spirit does this refinement, but gold is better purified so long as we feed the fire. Do not quench the refining fire of the Holy Spirit. Do not pour water on the fire by feeding your selfish desires.

Fire quenchers are things you may not even be aware of. Ask the Holy Spirit to reveal them to you. They can be idols like cars and sports, lusts of drinking and eating, pride in unforgiveness and money, or sins of disobedience like in not spreading the Gospel message or failing to pray.

The biggest sanctification killer is not reading the Word. The easiest way to quench the Spirit is not to put wood on the fire; it will go out rather quickly if you spend your time with the world's distractions instead of with God's living power charger.

The Holy Spirit is a living fire. He is working on the inside of you now, refining you like gold, if you let Him. But if you do not remain in His Word and cooperate with Him, you will be refined by fire on Judgment Day.[121] The more refinement you undertake now, the easier it will be to finish your sanctification on Judgment Day. You must be made holy, for that is the only way you can be in the presence of the Lord, which is the only place any of creation wants to be![122]

Once the joy and peace of the presence of the Lord is revealed to all mankind, there will be weeping upon weeping for those cast away from His presence.[123] You will be sanctified by the Faithful One, but if you choose to quench Him now, what will be the cost?

Choose not to know this cost, but choose obedience to the One who died to set us free and make us like Him! We are very imperfect, but the One who lives in us is perfect and working day-by-day to make us perfect, one choice at a time.

*God's Promise:*
You will be made holy and perfect whether you are ready or not; be well on your way in your sanctification process before that coming Day.

# Chosen to Be Saved

> But we ought always to thank God for you, brothers and sisters loved by the Lord, because God chose you as firstfruits to be saved through the sanctifying work of the Spirit and through belief in the truth. He called you to this through our gospel, that you might share in the glory of our Lord Jesus Christ. May our Lord Jesus Christ himself and God our Father, who loved us and by his grace gave us eternal encouragement and good hope, encourage your hearts and strengthen you in every good deed and word.
>
> —2 Thessalonians 2:13–14, 16–17 (NIV)

*Thank you, Lord, for choosing me and all those who believe in the name of Jesus Christ. Let me always be kind and gracious to those who do not believe, for they have not been chosen.*

*I do not know why You have chosen me, but I know that You have because You love me. I do not know why You love me, but I know You do because of what Jesus did to save me on Calvary. I know that I did nothing to be chosen, and I accept that there is nothing I can do to be saved now.*

*I know that I cannot share in the glory of Jesus unless I am made perfect, and I am thankful that I do not need to try to sanctify myself. Your precious Holy Spirit will sanctify me as I trust in your promises and have faith in your Word.*

*Help me then to spend more time in your Word so that the power of the Spirit can use truth to make me more like Jesus in body, soul, and spirit. I thank You that I will be sanctified and made like Jesus. I thank you that I will share in His reward, for His faithfulness to Your will and His obedience to the cross, that I might be saved by Your grace.*

*Sanctify me today, Father, so that I may show more love and benevolence to a people in need of light and hope. Do the work in me, which You promise to do, and make me more like Jesus so that the world would clearly see Him in me.*

*I am a simple and weak man, and I admit my need for constant encouragement and love from You, my heavenly Father. Give me Your Holy Spirit to know what to say, what to do, and how to carry myself through my day until Your work is done in and with me. Bless Your name. Thank you eternally. Amen.*

God's Promise:

You were chosen to share in Christ's eternal glory by God's good will, and grace now abounds in you to seal the promise to transform you into the image of Jesus.

# Life in Christ

> For through the law I died to the law
> so that I might live for God.
> I have been crucified with Christ
> and I no longer live, but Christ lives in me.
> The life I now live in the body,
> I live by faith in the Son of God,
> who loved me and gave himself for me.
> I do not set aside the grace of God,
> for if righteousness could be gained through
> the law, Christ died for nothing!
>
> —Galatians 2:19–21 (NIV)

Jesus paid it all for us on Calvary. He paid the penalty for all of our sins before we were ever born to break the chains of God's commandments.[124] For freedom's sake we are therefore set free from the law.[125]

If my relationship with God is dependent on my observance of the law, then Jesus died for nothing. However the law of sin and death no longer has power over me—I am therefore free to fearlessly serve God.[126]

Jesus carried the entirety my life with Him on the cross. We were with Him on the cross. We were chosen in Him before the foundation of the world.[127]

This is how He was able to pay for our sins and repair our shame, because we were held by Him on Calvary.

God gave His Spirit to every man when He breathed life into our bodies.[128] He poured our spirit into us out from heaven, down to earth, and into our body. From God we were born, but quickly died because of the law and its penalty when we sinned.[129]

Christ substituted Himself for me, took my penalty, and was crucified. Being chosen in Him, He was dead and buried along with my spirit. Since I was resurrected with Jesus, as soon as I believed Him and what He did for me, my spirit was made alive again by the power of His Holy Spirit, and God came to live in my heart, never to be corrupted again, for the law had been satisfied by Christ's death.

Now my life is no longer my own.[130] Christ living inside of me is now the reason I live and breathe. All this is so I can be free to serve God and love and do good works glorifying Him. It is pure grace that I ever lived and pure grace that I now live free to eternally praise and honor His holy name.

*God's Promise:*
You were crucified with Jesus. You now live with Jesus on the inside trying to shine outside. By faith in this promise, you are free to live a supernatural life of love.

# Father

> But when the set time had fully come, God sent his Son, born of a woman, born under the law, to redeem those under the law, that we might receive adoption to sonship. Because you are his sons, God sent the Spirit of his Son into our hearts, the Spirit who calls out, *"Abba*, Father." So you are no longer a slave, but God's child; and since you are his child, God has made you also an heir.
>
> —Galatians 4:4–7 (NIV)

We have been adopted by God the Father as sons and daughters and given the kingdom as joint heirs with Christ. Being adopted means that we were once someone else's child, and in fact, we were children of the devil.

As soon as we sinned, we obtained spiritual death for disobedience and were separated from the life-giving Spirit.[131] If a baby were spiritually dead upon birth because of his sinful parents, then Jesus would have been spiritually dead also. The flesh is sinful in nature, but it is our choice to commit the actual sin once reaching the age of accountability.

Jesus lived on earth fully man in sinful flesh

but with the Holy Spirit living inside of Him. Jesus was the holy Lamb of God—death therefore occurs when we sin, not when we are born.

Jesus was the son of God as the last Adam—unlike the first Adam, Christ did not sin and remained spiritually alive. Because Jesus had no sin, the Holy Spirit was allowed to unite us with Him on Calvary and place our sin in Christ, making His death legal by substitution. Through our unified spiritual death on the cross, we were legally adopted as sons and daughters of our Heavenly Father.

As children of disobedience, since sin was our master, the devil was our natural spiritual father.[132] But God rescued us from the devil's household through the work of Christ at no choice of our own. A little child does not ask to be adopted—they are just one of many lost in the orphanage when a savior extends a hand of mercy, pays a price, and brings them home. The adopted child is often brought home to live with natural children as equal and joint heirs.

God the Father reached down from heaven and pulled us out of the devil's orphanage and made us joint heirs with His Son Jesus. We have been made spiritually alive forever as sons and daughters through the atonement of the blood of the Lamb by the power Holy Spirit.

*God's Promise:*
Our spirit is now fused with the Holy Spirit, the gift for being saved in Christ, and we have the right to cry out to God as our loving and merciful Father.

# Faith through Love

> You who are trying to be justified by the law have been alienated from Christ; you have fallen away from grace. For through the Spirit we eagerly await by faith the righteousness for which we hope. For in Christ Jesus neither circumcision nor uncircumcision has any value. The only thing that counts is faith expressing itself through love. For the entire law is fulfilled in keeping this one command: "Love your neighbor as yourself."
>
> —Galatians 5:4–6, 14 (NIV)

Love has replaced the law. Righteousness by faith has replaced justification through works. God's grace is sufficient for your righteousness and worthiness to be called child by the Most High.

Jesus is grace to you—there is nothing you did to earn it and nothing you can do to keep it. All you can do is allow grace to sustain you by faith.

The law was done away with through the love God showed us on the cross. It was God's faith to His promise to set us free through the love of Jesus that saved us and gave us His righteousness. It is our choice, even once saved, to accept this grace by faith and allow Christ's righteousness to justify us. We must choose to allow His grace to sustain us.[133]

If we try to please God through works, we freely yoke ourselves back to the slavery of the law.[134] God is only pleased with us because of Jesus living inside of us—only Jesus, the innocent One dying for our sins, was able to please Holy God. The only thing that matters is our works done in love through faith in Jesus and God's promises.[135]

We must do good works because we love Jesus and for no other reason except to glorify His name. We bring honor to the Father as we love others as a living sacrifice. God is pleased with us when our heart is continually bent toward Him to serve Him in faith, live in His grace, and fulfill His will.

The Holy Spirit comforts us that God's grace is sufficient to provide all our needs. When the world begs us to return to bondage, He beckons us surrender to God's will and promises. Nothing in this life contributes to our acceptance by God except Jesus Christ.[136] We can only wait as God sanctifies us in Christ and hope for the day of perfection. So as it was with God's faithful display of love to us, it must be with us. Love your enemy. Love those who can offer you nothing. Love God's handiwork. Love God. By your life of love, your faith will accomplish everything that matters for the God who saved you.

*God's Promise:*
True faith in God's promises will express itself by your love for Jesus and zeal for His commandments.

# Crucified

> So I say, walk by the Spirit, and you will not gratify the desires of the flesh. For the flesh desires what is contrary to the Spirit, and the Spirit what is contrary to the flesh. They are in conflict with each other, so that you are not to do whatever you want. But if you are led by the Spirit, you are not under the law. Those who belong to Christ Jesus have crucified the flesh with its passions and desires.
>
> —Galatians 5:16–18, 24 (NIV)

Serving God with true good works has been proven impossible without the power of the Holy Spirit.[137] Even if we seem to be doing good works, apart from Jesus's will, we would only be doing them for ourselves, possibly in fear of judgment, but not out of love.

This is due to our flesh which was corrupted forever by Adam's sin. Our flesh is tainted with the sinful nature, which, by Satan's plan, gives us passions and desires naturally opposed to God's will.[138] Rebellion, disobedience, and self-gratification are all we can achieve on our own until Jesus plucks us from the tainted garden.

Once we are saved, the real struggle begins. Now we know to do good and are aware of the law but find ourselves unable to measure up and defeat sin.[139]

We wonder why we can't seem to defeat our sinful nature, and the guilt and shame we feel causes confusion, doubt, and dismay. We even feel like God is ashamed of us, but these emotions are only lies of the devil.

Jesus forgave all our sins and bore all our shame, so there is nothing to fear. Why, then, if our flesh was crucified with Christ, is it still so hard to defeat our sinful natures? Our flesh has been crucified, but look, it is still alive; it's not dead yet! However, it is nailed to the cross and has been defeated; yet it still has the power of spiteful and shameless will by nature.

We must not feed or water our flesh. We must claim the promise that our flesh has been nailed to the cross, has been permanently defeated, and that the Holy Spirit of God now lives in us to assure our victory. But we must let our flesh starve and die.

Walk in the Spirit: be kind, loving, patient, obedient, and have faith. Stop watching sex and violence; this feeds your flesh and makes it stronger. Stop reading books with no godly wisdom or value, and stop listening to music that does not honor God.

Instead, feed yourself with the living Word of God through daily Bible study. Pray on all occasions and with thanksgiving and purpose.[140] Know God's promises and claim them by faith daily.

As you daily walk in the Spirit in this way, your flesh will grow weaker and weaker, and soon, its crucified voice will become silent, the voice of God will sound like a song, and the fruit of the Spirit will abound with life.

What you feed grows stronger. Your flesh has been crucified; do not feed it as it hangs on the cross. Feed your new nature instead, which is a living spirit sustained by grace. Every word the flesh speaks is positioned against the Spirit. The promises of God, made effective by His own living Spirit inside of you, will give you victory over sin so that you may freely choose to love.

*God's Promise:*
Your flesh has been nailed to the cross with Jesus, and you no longer are required to obey its desires, for the Holy Spirit now rules in your heart.

# We Reap What We Sow

Do not be deceived: God cannot be mocked. A man reaps what he sows. Whoever sows to please their flesh, from the flesh will reap destruction; whoever sows to please the Spirit, from the Spirit will reap eternal life. Let us not become weary in doing good, for at the proper time we will reap a harvest if we do not give up.

—Galatians 6:7–9 (NIV)

We are free from the law but not free from the consequences of our actions. If we choose to serve our flesh and commit sin, we will give it what it desires, and that is destruction, for decay is all it knows.

There is nothing but death found in the nature of flesh. It is dying and reaps death.[141] Note that God does not repay sin with destruction for the believer; the flesh serves up destruction according to its own nature. The devil is an instigating and cheering audience in this battle. But we maintain free will to either feed our fleshy and selfish desires, or seek God and live in His grace, free to love like Jesus.

When we willingly sin, we reap consequences: loss, sickness, sadness, regret, guilt, shame, and everything else that is a result of man's fallen nature and opposed to the joy and peace of the Lord.[142] We must repent and leave our sin at the cross and pray for His mercy and restoration. He loves you enough to give you another day to choose Him.[143]

When we serve the Spirit with good works, we reap eternal life with blessings and rewards which are permanent. As a child of God, your good works are eternal and sustained by the same Spirit who sealed you forever as an heir with Christ.

Purpose your life against the world and the desires of self and in favor of God's love and perfect will for your life. Be sensitive to the cause of your situation, for most negative situations are a direct result of your flesh being strong enough to cause sin and reward you with destruction in some area of your life.

You may be surprised at just how many of your sins are a result of your flesh and not a direct cause of temptation by Satan.[144] Sow into God's work of saving lives and watch how the Spirit testifies to Jesus Christ in you. Life is not a mystery.

"Stuff" does not just happen. God's justice cannot be mocked. We reap what we sow. If we sow seeds into our selfish lives, we reap a harvest of loss. If we sow seeds into God's kingdom with purity of heart in excess of the seeds we might sow to our self, we will reap the fruit of the Spirit with eternal life enjoying eternal rewards.

But do not be dismayed. There is a reason for everything.[145] We either reap what we sow, or we are conquerors in Christ over the devil's attacks for God's glory.[146]

God's purpose is to make you like Jesus, first to do good works, then to be with you forever in holiness. Whenever you have pain or loss, don't claim "stuff" happens or cry "Why me?" Rather, seek God's face and hand in it. Either God wants you to see an area of your life where you need to change, or He wants to take control of the situation for His glory (typically both).

In any case, for a child of God, He wants to bear all your burdens as He sanctifies you in His Son.[147] Praise Him in the storm, and praise Him in the calm, for all things work for good to those who love Him and are called by His name.

*God's Promise:*
No good deed goes unrewarded for a child of God.

# The Mind of Christ

> The person with the Spirit makes judgments about all things, but such a person is not subject to merely human judgments, for, "Who has known the mind of the Lord so as to instruct him?" But we have the mind of Christ.
> —1 Corinthians 2:15–16 (NIV)

No one knows the thoughts of God except the Holy Spirit. The Holy Bible is a revelation of God to mankind so that we would have everything we would need to understand salvation and learn how to live a life of love in Jesus Christ.

If the Bible contained everything we needed from the mind of God to live, then the Holy Spirit would be of no use to us as all we would need to do is study the Bible and live through knowledge. But we know that to be a falsity, for the Pharisees and Jews who were "experts" in the law and Scriptures were but whitewashed tombs before God—they crucified the Son of God because they did not have the Spirit.[148]

The brief life of Jesus and all He said and did was said to exceed all that man could write down.[149] So how, then, can someone claim that the Spirit does not reveal new truth and understanding to people through discernment, wisdom, and revelation? Foolishness! The Holy Spirit gives us the mind of God, and to claim that all of God's knowledge, wisdom, and thoughts are fully contained in a single book is nonsense.

God is bigger in thoughts alone than can be measured.[150] Even so, every thought and revelation and must be taken captive to the mind of Christ, as already revealed to us in the Holy Bible, by the very Holy Spirit we desire to affirm as providing it, in order to discern the truth without error or confusion.

We have the mind of Christ. That does not mean all our thoughts are God's thoughts. In fact, the majority of my thoughts are fleshy garbage. But the Holy Spirit is speaking through the noise and revealing God's will day-by-day and showing the mystery of salvation through Christ in me.

The gift of discernment belongs to every believer in some measure, for it is the wisdom of God to know right and wrong, truth or lie, this or that. Every choice there is to make has a divine purpose.

People can say that God does not care whether we buy iceberg lettuce or romaine lettuce, but I beg to differ. God knows today which one may be clean and which one may have unhealthy bacteria. God knows which one will last longer in the refrigerator. God knows which one will taste better and bring more enjoyment. God knows which one will be more nutritious to us.

God knows everything and cares enough about us to help us in every decision. This does not mean that we should hold a prayer vigil in front of the veggie aisle, but it does mean that we should acknowledge His provision, protection, and grace.

Praying in the Spirit for God to guide you in all your daily decisions will result in the Holy Spirit leading you to choose the right lettuce. And if you learn to discern the little things, God will entrust you with the discernment of the big things. We have the mind of Christ. Let us walk in the Spirit, even for lettuce.

*God's Promise:*
No one knows the deep and hidden thoughts of God but the Holy Spirit; we have been given the very mind of Christ through the gift of His Spirit.

# One Way Out

> No temptation has overtaken you
> except what is common to mankind.
> And God is faithful; he will not let you
> be tempted beyond what you can bear.
> But when you are tempted, he will also
> provide a way out so that you can endure it.
>
> —1 Corinthians 10:13 (NIV)

Our God is faithful to His promises, and He promises to make a way for us to resist the devil's temptations. Man has been tempted into sin since Adam, and there is no temptation available to Satan that God does not know about and have dominion over.[151]

Jesus lived so that God the Son could experience firsthand all of the tools and flaming arrows of the devil, and He resisted them all. So God has triumphed over the devil's temptations for us, and by trusting in His power and grace, we can also resist them successfully.

We must, however, choose to desire Jesus and not the temporary pleasures of the flesh. To successfully serve our Lord, which is our reasonable duty for being saved from death,[152] we must first defeat our flesh and overcome the devil's tricks. To do this is impossible on our own. But good news! God is in control. All we have to do is yield our will to Him, and He will temper the devil's temptations and provide a way of escape.

God will replace the devil's temptations and the lust of the flesh with His peace and comfort. He will show us that choosing Him is always better for us than choosing sin; and by His grace, He will continue to sanctify us, not with guilt and shame, but with faith and hope.

Put your trust in Jesus to save you from the devil's deceit and lies, and He will deliver you from sin so you can follow Him freely and triumphantly in His perfect will.

*God's Promise:*
God is walking with you every step of the way and will show you how to resist temptation if you choose His love over the love of self.

# For the Common Good

> Now to each one the manifestation of the Spirit is given for the common good. To one there is given through the Spirit a message of wisdom, to another a message of knowledge by means of the same Spirit, to another faith by the same Spirit, to another gifts of healing by that one Spirit, to another miraculous powers, to another prophecy, to another distinguishing between spirits, to another speaking in different kinds of tongues, and to still another the interpretation of tongues. All these are the work of one and the same Spirit, and he distributes them to each one, just as he determines.
>
> —1 Corinthians 12:7–11 (NIV)

The gift of the Holy Spirit was bestowed upon you when you received salvation and were baptized into the body of Christ for eternity. Along with the other benefits of having God live inside of you is the promise that the Holy Spirit will manifest His presence in you with outward displays of power and glory: with faith, wisdom, knowledge, prophecy, discernment, miracles, and tongues.

The Holy Spirit actively determines, as a person of God, which, when, who, and why. We do not need to ask for them but are expected to be sensitive to His presence and cultivate our relationship with Him through His Word, and our gifts will blossom.

The Spirit distributes His gifts to each believer as He chooses. Some may have one, some all, yet to others, some at different times in our walk with Him. Know your gift, asking Him first to reveal it to you, and then seek His will as to what you are to do with your gift.

For certain, your gift is given for the common good of the body of Christ and not for yourself. Be humble but confident with your gifts, because they are a promise from God, and the very of God the Holy Spirit personally working out God's will through you.

Return all of this gift back to the church—someday you will be accountable for how you used the gifts of the Holy Spirit to do God's work of saving man and strengthening the body of Jesus Christ, all for the glory of the Father.

*God's Promise:*

Every believer has the Holy Spirit living on the inside of them from the moment of salvation, and He will confirm His presence through His supernatural gifts.

# Baptized

> Just as a body, though one, has many parts,
> but all its many parts form one body, so it is
> with Christ. For we were all baptized by one
> Spirit so as to form one body—whether Jews
> or Gentiles, slave or free—and we were all
> given the one Spirit to drink.
>
> —1 Corinthians 12:12–13 (NIV)

The Holy Spirit was given to all of us when God sent Him to baptize us into the body of Christ. There should be no question of that. Anyone who thinks that a person must be water-baptized to receive the initial gift of the Holy Spirit is unfortunately mislead.

Salvation is God's work. Baptism is also God's work. Water baptism is a work man does—albeit a good work, we cannot make God do anything by our own actions. It is only by faith that God can be pleased. It is by our faith, humility, and love that God is persuaded to move upon us and for us with power.

We can only exercise faith in His promises, and He promises that He gave us His Spirit when He baptized us into the body of Christ. This can only take place when Jesus chooses to turn a heart of stone into a heart of flesh by His blood. This is salvation by definition. If we are placed into the body of Christ, we will live forever, for Jesus will in no way lose us.[153]

The Holy Spirit can do what He likes with you, but He can be resisted. If we do not claim by faith His presence, we may not even notice it. But if we feed our soul with the Word of God and seek His presence, He will show up into our earthly experience.

The cup of the Spirit is bottomless, and we may drink up His presence unendingly. This is an action we can do: ask the Holy Spirit to fill you and overflow you with His presence and power to serve Jesus in love and glorify the Father.

To be saved but not filled with the Holy Spirit is like having a river flowing through your property but choosing to stand along the shore, claiming you are dirty and thirsty. It is in our power and authority to wade in the river, drink our fill and bathe in its cleansing flow, or freely sit on the shore, dry and thirsty.

You have the Spirit, so fill your soul with Him. The power of the river of life comes from within. Let the Spirit fill your soul and flow out of you into the world.

*God's Promise:*
You have had God the Spirit eternally placed and deeply rooted inside of you since the day you were saved.

# God Is Love

> If I speak in the tongues of men or of angels,
> but do not have love, I am only a resounding
> gong or a clanging cymbal. If I have the gift of
> prophecy and can fathom all mysteries and all
> knowledge, and if I have a faith that can move
> mountains, but do not have love, I am nothing.
> If I give all I possess to the poor and give over
> my body to hardship that I may boast, but do
> not have love, I gain nothing.
> Love never fails.
> But where there are prophecies,
> they will cease; where there are tongues,
> they will be stilled; where there is knowledge,
> it will pass away.
>
> —1 Corinthians 13:1–3, 8 (NIV)

God is love.[154] He has shown His love to us through creation. He created in Adam a desire to love and to be loved so great that He chose to share it with Eve. God knew His freely given love would be returned to Him in kind.

God has never forced anyone to love Him. Love is the one emotion that cannot be coerced. To love is purely a personal choice, and if one truly loves, they will put the recipient of that love before themselves and all other things.

God loved each man and woman ever created by creating them, knowing that most of them would not love Him in return. But He loved us anyway, and even though we rejected Him, He chose to give us good gifts and glory in the love we share for each other, our pets, and His creation, whether we acknowledge Him for it or not. That is truly selfless and gracious love.

Since He is the origin of life and love, He enjoys our ability to freely love and be loved and is all the more glorified when we choose to freely love Him in return. The love He gave all of mankind will be revealed to all on Judgment Day, and for this reason, every knee shall bow when we see God as the origin and manifestation of all love.

God's perfect display of love to us was on the cross. He loved us so greatly that despite our disobedience, He chose the nails so we could be with Him forever, in perfect love. He paid the penalty for everyone's sins and died a horrific death because of His unchangeable love for each us, whether or not we would ever recognize Him as our Savior.[155]

Everything God does or has done for mankind has been rooted in His love for mankind. Even when justice and judgment are pronounced, it is rooted in love. We discipline our children because we love them, even though they don't see it that way. God cannot operate toward mankind without His actions being rooted in love, because He is love.

God is also perfectly just in His judgment; where love and justice meet, only God can perfect both, because He is perfect.[156] Perfect love compelled God the Son to die on a Roman cross. Perfect love compels God to offer salvation to all, but not force it on anyone—perfect love allows free will to reign in our lives as God desires that we be sovereign like Him. So our promise here is that love never fails, because God is love, and God never fails. Everything else on this earth will pass away: prophecies, knowledge, and all the expressions of creation. All that will remain is the love we have shown each other.

When we love others sacrificially like Paul explains in 1 Corinthians 13:4–7, we are unstoppable forces in this world. Every deed we do, every step we take, and every word we speak, if done because of our love for someone else and Jesus Christ living in them, it will succeed in its eternal design.

*God's Promise:*
The keystone to living a life of love is a having a heart of flesh—if you desire to live an extraordinary life in Christ you must have a heart rooted in love for your neighbor and deeply in love with your Lord.

# Grace

> But by the grace of God I am what I am, and his grace to me was not without effect. No, I worked harder than all of them—yet not I, but the grace of God that was with me.
>
> —1 Corinthians 15:10 (NIV)

Paul knew he was saved by grace because his sin was mature the day Christ transformed his heart on the road to Damascus. Saul did everything in his own power to choose hell, working to kill out Jesus's life on earth within the children of God, desiring even to crucify Christ Himself again if it were possible.

There is only one Gospel.[157] God does not save people by any other way. So Saul's conversion is a perfect representation of how all believers are saved: by grace alone.

One moment we are going in a direction perfectly opposed to God, and in an instant, the Holy Spirit moves within us, turns our heart of stone to flesh, takes up permanent residence, and turns us in a new direction wholly positioned for heaven. Then, by faith, we accept what Scripture says about Jesus and what God says happened to us and is our new destiny.

As there was nothing Saul did to be chosen by God and saved, so there was nothing, not a thing, we did to deserve being saved. It was God's grace alone that chose us in Christ to be saved.

There are not multiple Gospels but only one, and the Gospel that saved Saul and changed him to Paul is the one that took you from death to life: the Gospel of Jesus Christ and God's grace. But we know why this Gospel of grace saved us! So that we would become coworkers with God, sharing the message of love, glorifying His name because of grace.

It is not in our own ability but by His grace alone we are to do His work.[158] If we try to do good works in our own ability, then they are not God's works, but our own works. Only God's works have eternal value. Remember daily, it is grace that saved you and grace that gives you life.

*God's Promise:*
Grace saved you, and grace sustains you. The Holy Spirit is this grace.

# Our Hope

> I face death every day—yes, just as surely as I boast about you in Christ Jesus our Lord. If I fought wild beasts in Ephesus with no more than human hopes, what have I gained? If the dead are not raised, "Let us eat and drink, for tomorrow we die."
> —1 Corinthians 15:31–32 (NIV)

Our hope is in Christ, for our faith rests in the fact that God raised Him from the dead.[159] If Christ were still in the tomb, then what hope would we have? But not only was He raised, but he lived among the brethren for over a month, preaching this good news so that we would believe this extraordinary miracle![160]

The power of God is without limit. He is not bound by time. If God can make a man out of a two-cell embryo, then He can take our dead body and make it new. Time does not control God's ability or persuade His work.

Too many Christians live like this world is their place of joy, but this is the deception of the devil. Christ's presence is our place of joy. This life is but a whisper of what life in God's presence will be like.

## Paul's Comfort

And we will have our bodies back, without pain and fleshy desires, to enjoy our life with Christ.

It is tragic, but grace-sustained, that believers fail to go all-in for Christ and instead, hold onto this world's pleasures for fear of the unknown. The grand celebration is not to be had here; it is to be had there in heaven. Now is the time to work. There will be a time when there will be no need for work, as the sick, poor, and lost—even death itself—will be gone.[161]

Paul's comfort in the resurrection of the dead fueled his passion to serve the Gospel. He feared no man, no pain, and no death, for he feared God alone. His faith in God's ability and promise to raise him from the dead assured him that God could and would protect him from death until he fulfilled God's complete will.

Not stoning to death, or being thrown into the arena with killer beasts, could curtail Paul's faith in God's ability to protect him while he served Christ. We don't know the details of this story, but the wild beasts Paul fought in Ephesus were likely more afraid of Paul than he was of them, for Paul had Christ in full measure fighting his battles for him.

This is not a time to eat, drink, shop, golf, and serve yourself in excess. Eternity will be your time to be rewarded for good works, if you have them. But if all you did was be lazy and complacent around here with respect to good works, then you have your reward, and what will be the cost on Judgment Day for you?[162]

We must look to the cross for the purpose of our salvation: to love others with all our heart and wealth.

Then we must look to the empty tomb for our promise of hope: life eternally spent with Christ in heaven. Then we can go and live an extraordinary life doing good works for the One who saved us, called us, and promised us this hope and blessed assurance.

*God's Promise:*

Life as God originally planned will only begin when you die, so don't lose any part of it by living for this world; instead, live fully for earning your inheritance in the world to come.

# Stand Firm

> Therefore, my dear brothers and sisters,
> stand firm. Let nothing move you.
> Always give yourselves fully to the work of
> the Lord, because you know that your labor
> in the Lord is not in vain.
>
> —1 Corinthians 15:58 (NIV)

We have the promise of eternal life with a new, resurrected, and perfect body and will have forever to enjoy our rewards for doing good works.[163] With this promise in our heart, Paul commands us to stand firm and let nothing move us from fully committing our lives to doing the work of God. Let nothing move us from the path of following Jesus, because we have the promise that all our work for God will not be without great reward when we get to heaven.

We must first understand what the work of God is, and then seek His will for our lives in alignment with His work. There is neither a man nor woman saved who has not been specifically chosen by God to do good works.[164] He has equipped you to do this work with His Holy Spirit.

We are so helpless to do good on our own in this

fallen world that God found it mandatory to live inside of us, doing the good works through us.[165] But we must cooperate. We still have permissive free will to choose to follow Jesus or follow the ways of the world, seeking self-fulfillment.[166]

Jesus desires that we are filled by His Spirit, not by the world. He has called us out of this world but has not forced us out as long as we still have breath.[167]

To know the work of God, we must read the Bible. God's work is to save man through the call of love.[168] We are called to be that love.

*God's Promise:*

Do good works because of the love of Jesus in you, and Jesus will personally reward you for each and every good deed.

# The Purpose of Comfort

> Praise be to the God and Father of our Lord Jesus Christ, the Father of compassion and the God of all comfort, who comforts us in all our troubles so that we can comfort those in any trouble with the comfort we ourselves receive from God. For just as we share abundantly in the sufferings of Christ, so also does our comfort abound through Christ. If we are distressed, it is for your comfort and salvation; if we are comforted, it is for your comfort, which produces in you patient endurance of the same sufferings we suffer.
>
> —2 Corinthians 1:3–6 (NIV)

If there was ever a man who suffered for the sake of the Lord, it was Paul.[169] He wrote this hope and encouragement to the Corinthians to give them the promise of the comfort of God which he experienced through in his sufferings. Paul had gone through so much persecution in Asia that living brought him despair, and the belief that he would soon die seemed his only hope and comfort. But instead of despair, he turned to God for help, and God gave Paul and his companions peace and joy in their sufferings, a joy that would cause a man to sing praises to God even while being beaten to death.[170]

We have this comfort because of God's mercy. Jesus suffered alone. He did not have any comfort as He was tortured and crucified, at least nothing like the comfort we now have because of His substitution. Jesus suffered the wrath of God for us and died as a curse. We benefit from His death with grace in the peace of God and in Christ's imputed righteousness.

God's anger was turned against Jesus on our behalf. The only comfort Christ had was the knowledge that He was doing the will of the Father and that after it would be finished. By faith alone Jesus would need to believe that He would live again and reign forever, and this time with His beloved by His side: us.

Jesus had the comfort of hope in the promises of His Father, but this is not the same as the comfort Paul speaks of. Paul's comfort is the very presence of God. Jesus was left to die without Paul's comfort so that God could give Paul His Holy Spirit through Christ's faith, love, and obedience.[171]

We are to clearly understand what Jesus did for us on Calvary was so that the Holy Spirit could come to us and live in us. If we truly understood the agony of the Son of God being separated from God the Father, all so that we could be saved by grace, we would turn our back on the world and rush into the comforting arms of God.

It is to be our joy to suffer for the sake of the

Gospel.[172] Jesus did not go through His passion just to make us feel better or make us better than others. No, He suffered so that we would join Him in holy matrimony to share in His work: the work of saving lives.

Let us be comforted by His Spirit as we suffer affliction because we are following Jesus in love. He did not intend for us to be comforted because of suffering due to our unrepentant sin, although He is good enough in His grace to do it. Grace and mercy cover our sin-debt; His love belongs to us to live a holy and righteous life. We must not confuse suffering due to sin with suffering due to following Christ.

Comfort those following Christ with the comfort you have received. Correct those following the world with the Fatherly correction you once knew. Live fully for Christ and the sake of the Gospel of peace, and you will know the full comfort of the loving embrace of the Father through the indwelling presence of His Holy Spirit.

*God's Promise:*

The purpose of God's comfort is to give us endurance while following Jesus and doing good works.

# Amen

> For no matter how many promises God has made, they are "Yes" in Christ. And so through him the "Amen" is spoken by us to the glory of God. Now it is God who makes both us and you stand firm in Christ. He anointed us, set his seal of ownership on us, and put his Spirit in our hearts as a deposit, guaranteeing what is to come.
> —2 Corinthians 1:20–22 (NIV)

"In Jesus's name we pray, Amen."

This is why we say what we say and do what we do, because all of the promises of God are fulfilled in and through Christ. It is Christ alone who bridged the infinite gap between God's holiness and man's sinful nature. It is only through Christ that we can even pray to God and have Him hear our plea.[173] It is only through Christ that we can claim any of the promises God gave us in the Bible, and by Jesus's holy name, we can claim every one for ourselves and live a supernatural life of faith doing extraordinary things in love.

Because of Jesus, we say "Amen" and "Hallelujah." Praise be to the Father for the gift. All for me so that the work He does in me by His goodwill brings Him honor and glory. My love of Jesus is the proof that He lives in me. I have been given all things—an inheritance in glory and perfection. Every good thing comes from the Father as I seek to know His will, His love, and His Son.[174]

Here I am, Lord. Let Your love wash over me and into this world, which You died to save. Not I but Christ. Every good thing, every word of your Holy Bible, and everything I do for You is a result of Christ in me, as Your Spirit testifies in me. All this through Jesus and by no other name or way. I thank You Father eternally. In Jesus's name we pray, Amen.

*God's Promise:*
God owns your life because He put His Spirit inside of you, sealing you with a guarantee of "Yes" and "Amen" in Christ.

## Competence

> Such confidence we have through Christ before God. Not that we are competent in ourselves to claim anything for ourselves, but our competence comes from God. He has made us competent as ministers of a new covenant—not of the letter but of the Spirit; for the letter kills, but the Spirit gives life.
>
> —2 Corinthians 3:4–6 (NIV)

Too many Christians live without a care for the knowledge of the Holy Spirit. But the Spirit still lives inside of them, sealing them with holiness for the day of redemption.[175] He comforts, convicts, and protects nonetheless. Even though people change and ignore the indwelling presence and work of the Holy Spirit, He does not change, nor does He leave.[176]

Too many Christians do not see the value in studying the Bible. To them, it is not a living Word but a book of stories that only needs to be read once, or not at all, just heard about on Sundays from the preacher. To them, the Spirit does not speak; yet He speaks first through the Word, by application and appreciation, rooted from one's desire to know Christ and the heart of God.[177]

Too many Christians believe the Word of God is dead, no longer living, breathing, or speaking to us today. They will say that there is no more revelation from God, that He no longer speaks to us, or that the Bible is closed and finished with respect to God's mind, truth, and heart. But how could any book be said to contain all there is to know about our limitless God? Only eternity could be enough to know about the mysteries of God.

Not enough Christians call out to the Holy Spirit to speak to their heart as they meditate on the Word of God. Be still and know that He is God, and search His Word for His Truth. The Holy Spirit does not speak apart from the revealed Word of God.[178]

Christ is our competence. Let nothing be puffed up in us, but let all knowledge and wisdom be supplied directly from Him. We should seek, ask, and knock, and He will reward us with the wisdom and knowledge we seek from Him and seek to share. Let our competence be the Spirit's persuasion.

*God's Promise:*
The Word is alive. He lives, moves, and speaks to us in alignment with His nature revealed in the written Word, but He cannot be fully contained by simple sinful man.

# The Glory of God

> Now the Lord is the Spirit,
> and where the Spirit of the Lord is,
> there is freedom.
> And we all,
> who with unveiled faces
> contemplate the Lord's glory,
> are being transformed
> into his image
> with ever-increasing glory,
> which comes from the Lord,
> who is the Spirit.
>
> —2 Corinthians 3:17–18 (NIV)

The glory of the Lord is His magnificence and great beauty; it is the honor, praise, and worship due Him for what He has done.

The glory of the Lord is the awe we have for everything He has done and promises to do.

God is holy and glorious, and He deserves our praise just for being who He is and for what He has done as the Creator.[179]

But we have the cross to contemplate as we are being made like Him with the same glory He has. The living Holy Spirit is the glory of the Lord, and He is inside of us, transforming us into the very image of Christ so that we could be as He is in His glory.

What Jesus did for us on the cross—the redemption, the love, the victory—all this glory is being poured into us.

*God's Promise:*
The embodiment of the glory of Christ is the Spirit of the Lord, and He lives inside of us with the goal of making us like Jesus.

# Live the Gospel

> For what we preach is not ourselves, but Jesus Christ as Lord, and ourselves as your servants for Jesus' sake. All this is for your benefit, so that the grace that is reaching more and more people may cause thanksgiving to overflow to the glory of God. Therefore we do not lose heart. Though outwardly we are wasting away, yet inwardly we are being renewed day by day. For our light and momentary troubles are achieving for us an eternal glory that far outweighs them all.
>
> —2 Corinthians 4:5, 15–17 (NIV)

The foundational Gospel message for the world to hear is that Jesus Christ is Lord of all.[180]

If one accepts the Gospel, then he or she accepts that Jesus is Lord of their life. If Jesus is Lord of their life, then they obey Him.[181] If they obey Him, they follow Him.[182] If they follow Him, they leave everything else behind to do so and give everything over to Jesus.[183] They no longer live for themselves but for others as servants, loving people because they are loved.[184] They have committed their time, finances, talents, resources, skills, and bodies to serve the kingdom of God.

This is the Gospel message: Jesus Christ is Lord.[185] Does your life song preach the Gospel message that Jesus is Lord of your life? What do we have to fear? Nothing.[186] God did not give us a spirit of fear but a spirit of hope.[187]

Those who hold on to this life shall lose it, but those who give it away shall gain everlasting life filled with eternal glory and rewards.[188] Any sacrifice made to serve God will become a blessing.

It is for our good and benefit that Jesus calls us to be servants and follow Him, spreading the Gospel by doing good works. We reap a reward of brothers and sisters to praise and bless the name of Jesus when He calls us home. Any actual trouble that may come our way for following Jesus as Lord will become joy, for the very presence of God is made real as we bear the yoke of the death of Christ in us for the sake of life in Him.[189]

Paul followed Jesus as Lord and obeyed Him. He was troubled for certain, but he soon learned that God's presence in him while he was troubled was so immensely more enjoyable than the conflict that he was joyful to go through it for Jesus's sake. Jesus willingly went to the cross for us and asks us now to trust in Him and His promises by following Him.

Eternal glory is your reward for any momentary trouble that may come your way. You will never know what it means to truly live until you die to self and let Jesus become Lord of your life.

The world is a liar. Its ways do not bring joy; satisfying self does not bring happiness. There is no peace in disobedience.[190] Joy, peace, and happiness can only be found in Christ and can only be truly appreciated if you are following Him as Lord.[191]

Become a servant of those who need more than you. Be the love of the Father to a fatherless child. Be the peace of God to a poor widow. Be the Savior to a homeless man. Be the power of the Spirit of God to a world in need of the truth. Be Jesus.

*God's Promise:*
The glory of God is revealed in us as we proclaim the good news of hope in Jesus Christ.

# Life

> For while we are in this tent, we groan and are burdened, because we do not wish to be unclothed but to be clothed instead with our heavenly dwelling, so that what is mortal may be swallowed up by life. Now the one who has fashioned us for this very purpose is God, who has given us the Spirit as a deposit, guaranteeing what is to come.
> —2 Corinthians 5:4–5 (NIV)

We were baptized into the body of Christ when we were saved by the Holy Spirit.[192] God gave the Spirit to us as a down payment that we could hold on to as we long for our guaranteed future: a new body and a new life.

Yes, we are burdened with this life because we live in a fallen world corrupted by sin. If we desire the life that is truly life, we will ache with longing for our new heavenly body and new life. If we long for heaven, we will continually look toward heaven in anticipation, and with the cross as our viewpoint as we long to meet Jesus.

But many do not desire the things of heaven. The Bible is the living Word of God, our message from heaven, made alive in us by the Holy Spirit within us, yet many Christians shut Him up so they can have the pleasures of this life and not feel the conviction of disobedience.

Which life do you desire? Is this Spirit's guarantee your comfort, or is your comfort in the world's pleasures? Seek the life that is truly life and learn what it means to truly live today.

*God's Promise:*

God has made us to receive a new heavenly body and given us His Spirit to prepare our hearts to wear it forever.

# Balance Due

> So we make it our goal to please him, whether we are at home in the body or away from it. For we must all appear before the judgment seat of Christ, so that each of us may receive what is due us for the things done while in the body, whether good or bad.
>
> —2 Corinthians 5:9–10 (NIV)

There is nothing like the presence of our God. Once you seek the face of God to the point where He comes to you and fills you with His holy presence, you will never be the same. It is what drives men to leave everything and preach the Gospel in hostile nations.

We long to be in His presence forever. It is the only thing that can satisfy our longings. No longer can the things of this world satisfy us. A ten-second touch from Jesus will leave you spending the rest of your earthly life seeking His touch again, longing to please. All He wants is your heart.[193]

Once you are following Him by His Spirit, in His will, and doing His work, you are doing good. There is no other way to accomplish eternally good works than by allowing Christ Jesus to do them through us for His glory.[194]

If you are not following Jesus, you are not doing good works. If you are not doing good works, you are either doing bad works or works of non-effect. To know to do good and not to do it is sin.[195]

Following Jesus in love is a commandment.[196] You will be judged as either an obedient or disobedient believer.[197] Do not lose any of the crowns that await the obedient child of God!

*God's Promise:*

We follow Jesus not because of the promise of judgment, but because we long to please Him and be comforted by His presence.

# Purpose

> For Christ's love compels us, because we are convinced that one died for all, and therefore all died. And he died for all, that those who live should no longer live for themselves but for him who died for them and was raised again. We are therefore Christ's ambassadors, as though God were making his appeal through us. We implore you on Christ's behalf: Be reconciled to God.
>
> —2 Corinthians 5:14–15, 20 (NIV)

Let us be reminded of the purpose for our salvation. When we were saved, the Holy Spirit baptized us into the body of Christ forever. To do this, we were first baptized into His death. Our sins were nailed to the cross in Jesus, and we died to self and the power of sin. We were then buried with Christ and miraculously resurrected with new eternal life in Christ.

Before we could know it, we were given new life in Christ by the Holy Spirit living inside of us.[198] We now have a living spirit instead of a dead one, a spirit that has been resurrected by the very presence of God so that we would commune with Him and return to Him.

This is a promise of what Christ did for you on the cross and on Easter Sunday that you would be returned to His presence by grace. All this so that you would no longer choose to live for yourself but live for Christ who suffered and died to give you life.[199]

When you were saved, God forced His grace, mercy, and love on you by the power of the blood of Jesus. However, He did not take from you His greatest gift: free will.[200] He always gives us the choice to love Him for what He has done, or love the world for what it can do.[201]

The unsaved choose to hate God with various miscellaneous excuses, even though creation beckons them to love Him.[202] Many saved choose to hate God too because His cross is not desirable to bear, even though without the cross, they would suffer eternal punishment.[203]

You cannot serve both the world and God; you will necessarily love one and hate the other.[204] The life that truly demonstrates a pure love for God will desire nothing the world can provide, making available to God's kingdom everything in their possession. Yet in recognition of God's abundant blessings, this life will be thankful for God's provision while recognizing that the Lord who gives can also take away according to His purposes and for our benefit.

Blessings are gifts God provides, which we can enjoy while we fully seek His will. Worldly desires are pleasures we fulfill with money and time spent on self instead of the end being God's glory and purpose. The difference between a blessing from God and a selfish desire is impossible to determine unless we are walking in the Spirit doing His will. The Holy Spirit will convict us of these things; that is His job and promise.[205]

We must be reconciled to God. We must follow Him and do the same works of love and mercy He did. We are ambassadors for Christ. We must use our office to represent heaven on earth and not abuse it to satisfy self when eternal satisfaction awaits just a breath away.

We beg you, for your benefit and reward, live for Christ by faith. He is alive and stands at the door and says, "Come, I have only good things planned for you, if you would trust Me, and follow."[206]

*God's Promise:*

If you are saved, you died, were resurrected, and are called from the grave to live a new life unto God by following Jesus.

# Purity

> Therefore, since we have these promises, dear friends, let us purify ourselves from everything that contaminates body and spirit, perfecting holiness out of reverence for God.
>
> —2 Corinthians 7:1 (NIV)

Paul's comfort was in the promises of God. They were written on his heart by the Holy Spirit. He had the knowledge of the Old Testament prophets from his schooling but was given open-eyed wisdom to take the Word of God and apply it through love.

As believers, we are called to be different.[207] Our call to good works must begin in us and how we conduct ourselves. Sanctification is not complete upon salvation; it only begins there and is completed when we are clothed with our new heavenly body.[208] We are no longer required to observe the law as a condition of acceptance or judgment but out of respect and honor for the call of God.[209]

We must be different, showing reverence for God who made us to be a temple for His living presence.[210] I am not there yet, but at least I know where I desire to be—in a place where God is always pleased with my behavior as His son.

I desire to be separated, yet I am here in this world, by design or consequence, so I must love my way out by following Jesus. While my daily life brings me interaction with the unsaved at work, let them see Christ in me. While I lay myself down as a servant, let the church see Christ in me, not because I am good, or even do good, but because I desire to be holy and pure, even when I struggle just like them.

Let us purify ourselves from the sin and poor choices we have made and become like Christ. The Holy Spirit is helping us fight against our flesh through love. The flesh is powerful to sin, weak to do good.[211] We must yield ourselves to His purifying presence, which is our reasonable duty, out of reverence for God and what our holy and perfect Savior did for us on the cross.[212]

We are not holy when we think we do not sin—we all sin else we call God a liar. We are made holy because of the blood of Jesus; we are becoming holy as we follow Jesus. We are pure when our heart desires only what God desires. We are pure when our love for the world Jesus died to save is selfless. We are pure when we live according to the will of the Spirit.

*God's Promise:*

God has called us to be in the world, but not of the world, and to behave like good children who respect the wishes of their living Father.

# Brotherhood

> For when we came into Macedonia, we had no rest, but we were harassed at every turn—conflicts on the outside, fears within. But God, who comforts the downcast, comforted us by the coming of Titus, and not only by his coming but also by the comfort you had given him. He told us about your longing for me, your deep sorrow, your ardent concern for me, so that my joy was greater than ever.
>
> —2 Corinthians 7:5–7 (NIV)

Separation and isolation are the devil's great tools for attacking Christians with doubt and fear.[213] God gave us a Spirit of unity in the body of Christ for comfort and edification.

Anyone who willfully and inexcusably forgoes the gathering of the brethren in church has been separated by the devil. Church is not alone in front of the TV; it is not alone on a trout stream; it is not found doing Bible study at home. Church is finding joy and comfort in the body of Christ while praising God.[214]

Paul was greatly comforted just by hearing through Titus that the brethren in Corinth still cared about him. It was enough joy to comfort him in his great strife in

*Paul's Comfort*

Macedonia, building a longing in his heart to embrace his fellow Christians as if embracing the Son of God Himself.

Jesus prayed that we would be one just as He and the Father are One.[215] Fight back against the devil's attempts to keep you home and away from church gatherings. You need to be encouraged by your brothers and sisters in Christ, and they need you just the same. We are not left here on this earth to have a single relationship with God through the Bible and television; we are left here to unify within the body of Christ and spread the Gospel message through works of love.

God said He would save, but Jesus told us to make disciples. We cannot obey this command by allowing the devil to isolate us. Rise up and go; look hopeful to receiving joy and comfort. Are you looking to comfort others as well?

We all need each other, and it starts with you fighting for the hearts and lives of the brothers and sisters around you. We are all one in Christ. No one is better than the other; we all have the righteousness of Christ and the ability to love like Jesus. Let us be one so that we all may be strong in comfort in our days of trouble, which are sure to come.[216]

*God's Promise:*
We are better together today, tomorrow, and forever.

# Cheerful

Remember this: Whoever sows sparingly will also reap sparingly, and whoever sows generously will also reap generously. Each of you should give what you have decided in your heart to give, not reluctantly or under compulsion, for God loves a cheerful giver. And God is able to bless you abundantly, so that in all things at all times, having all that you need, you will abound in every good work.

—2 Corinthians 9:6–8 (NIV)

The law of life is of sowing and reaping. It is a condition of free will and a God-honoring promise. God desires our freewill offering to Him. The more we give, the more He will give back, guaranteed. But we must give out of the joy to give back to God. He first gave us undeserved blessings, and it is our choice whether we hold on to them or cheerfully give it back.

God knows what we have need of and is able to abundantly bless us with what we need, such that we will never be without that which we need.[217] What then do we need? We only need that which allows us to follow Jesus doing the good works appointed us.[218]

We are saved to do good works, and our cheerful freewill offering is our part to play. We must give our whole self over to Christ in service. This takes place internally, dying spiritually to self with Jesus on the cross. Then we must put our money where our mouth is and sow cheerfully by sacrifice into God's kingdom, thereby exercising our giving muscle, which strengthens our faith.[219]

We can stop eating cookies because we want to get in shape, but it is not until we get up and exercise that we get strong. Of course it hurts, but as you exercise your giving muscle, God demonstrates His faithfulness in what you are blessed with, and it soon becomes easy to give. Even if the blessings are not readily observable, we can be assured by God's promise that it is blessing us in both eternal and unseen ways.

We're not talking about your tithe here. That already belongs to God, so you had better be giving your 10 percent, cheerfully or not, or that is simple disobedience. We're talking about a cheerful freewill offering of any and all of the remaining 90 percent, plus your whole life in service to the God who saved you, in faith and love to His Word. He shall bless you abundantly as you do so.

*God's Promise:*
God, the Giver of all good things, loves cheerful and faithful givers, and will bless them abundantly in return. One cannot out-give God.

# Divine Power

> For though we live in the world, we do not wage war as the world does. The weapons we fight with are not the weapons of the world. On the contrary, they have divine power to demolish strongholds. We demolish arguments and every pretension that sets itself up against the knowledge of God, and we take captive every thought to make it obedient to Christ.
>
> —2 Corinthians 10:3–5 (NIV)

Paul's comfort was in the power of the Holy Spirit to convict men of truth and enact righteous judgment. His comfort was in the authority of Christ living inside of him, giving his words divine power to cause demons to flee and the devil himself to bow down to the cross of his defeat.

The truth will set you free.[220] For every argument and every thought ever generated by the mind of a man or angel, there is either yes or no in Christ. There are no gray areas with God; there is only truth, and that truth is His Word, and His Word is Jesus.

We are not to win arguments for Christ as if the truth needed to be defended. We are to demolish arguments.

Not engaging in an argument defuses its power. Responding to the falsity of foolishness with words of love and forgiveness renders man's wisdom folly in the light of the cross.

Jesus did not speak at the accusations of His accusers unless they first spoke of truth.[221] He did not argue, for they could not see the light of truth unless the Spirit opened their eyes.

We have the Spirit but cannot make Him move. We can only respond to what He is already doing.[222] If we see Him move in the hearts of men, let us rejoice! But who are we to determine who is worthy of seeing the truth of Jesus or not? It is God who draws men unto salvation in Christ. We are to be the message He uses.

Arguments and defenses against wrong only defend self; Christ needs no defense. Strength in silence, confidence in love, power in forgiveness—these are the weapons with which we fight and conquer every thought for Christ.

The Truth is the truth, and nothing changes Him. It cannot be conquered, and it cannot be hidden. The Holy Spirit is our sword's power, for He makes the Word of God effective in our war against the spirits of darkness. Know the Word, use Him carefully, and never fear the ramifications of speaking the truth.

*God's Promise:*
We have divine power to make every thought obedient to the truth of Jesus Christ.

# Masquerade

> And I will keep on doing what I am doing in order to cut the ground from under those who want an opportunity to be considered equal with us in the things they boast about. For such people are false apostles, deceitful workers, masquerading as apostles of Christ. And no wonder, for Satan himself masquerades as an angel of light. It is not surprising, then, if his servants also masquerade as servants of righteousness. Their end will be what their actions deserve.
> —2 Corinthians 11:12–15 (NIV)

Let my words be tested by fire and light. Let me boast in the Gospel of Jesus Christ. Let all thoughts and words be separated into truths by the prism of the cross. Let me always be able to discern false gospel from truth, liars from apostles, deceivers from lovers of Christ.

The church is rampant with false gospel preaching—rampant! It is the believers who allow it because they are ignorant of the truth and desire only spoon-fed Gospel and feel-good sermons. They forget that the devil prowls like a lion, seeking those whom he may devour.[223]

False doctrine devours life in Christ. When we allow the devil to feed us half-truths and seeds of doubt, we fall from grace. We are responsible to make every thought obedient to the mind of Christ. And we have the Bible to do this! The Corinthians had only a few letters, so Paul fought for their hearts and minds to know the truth as revealed in him.

There is only one Gospel. There is only one Christ. God does not author confusion concerning the truth—the devil does.[224] The Holy Spirit does not find it difficult to speak clearly to those who will listen through the Word.

If we will make our thoughts subject to the mind of Christ, the Holy Spirit will give us the truth we seek. But do you actually seek Him, or do you want the Bible to agree with your doctrine? Or worse yet, are you so filled with knowledge that you no longer desire the foundational Word of God? Pride hides the truth, but humility finds wisdom.[225]

If there were masqueraders penetrating the church in Corinth with false doctrine, how much more can we be guaranteed that they are here among us today? We know they are here, but there are so many false gospels out there it seems we all have one that makes us comfortable. The Gospel is not designed to make us feel comfortable! It is designed to separate us from this world and make us followers of Jesus until our day of perfection![226]

The Gospel message is life in Christ, not life in this world. The Gospel message is salvation by grace to do good works, not salvation by grace maintained by good works, and certainly not salvation by merit.[227]

Any preacher, teacher, or author who has a message not consistent with the whole of Scripture must have their message refined by the Holy Spirit. God does still speak, and no book is the exhaustible revelation of God (only eternity can sufficiently reveal God to us). But the Bible is perfect, and all knowledge and wisdom must be tested and supported by the written Word.

The Holy Spirit has been given to us so we would not be responsible for this on our own. But we must seek wisdom and know the Word so that we can defend the truth with the sword of the Spirit.[228]

I desire never to speak a gospel other than Christ and Christ crucified and glorified in me.[229] I will not temper the Gospel message to earn followers or profit. The Gospel is pure, powerful, and will span time into eternity. It is not I, but truth. Let the pieces fall by God's perfect judgment where they may, in mercy, in love, and for His glory.

*God's Promise:*

Satan and his legion of fallen angels and demons masquerade amongst the church as angels of light, seeking whom they may deceive and devour. The only way to know them is to know the truth, know your God, and seek the Holy Spirit's wisdom.

# Strength in Weakness

> Therefore, in order to keep me from becoming conceited, I was given a thorn in my flesh, a messenger of Satan, to torment me. Three times I pleaded with the Lord to take it away from me. But he said to me, "My grace is sufficient for you, for my power is made perfect in weakness." Therefore I will boast all the more gladly about my weaknesses, so that Christ's power may rest on me. That is why, for Christ's sake, I delight in weaknesses, in insults, in hardships, in persecutions, in difficulties. For when I am weak, then I am strong.
>
> —2 Corinthians 12:7b–10 (NIV)

God chooses imperfect men to be entrusted with the perfect Gospel. The truth is too powerful for a sinful man to bear, because pride and selfishness are our natural characteristics—rooted in darkness, they choose to hide from the light. This is why the Holy Spirit living inside of us and a brand new imputed nature is required to be able to bear the truth.

We are burdened with weaknesses so we would know, without a doubt, if we are found strong in the things of God, it is because of Christ in us and not at all because of us. The Holy Spirit comforts us with an inner grace-embrace and makes us strong in Christ in our weakness.

The true Gospel will be marked clearly with the preaching and teaching of "not I but Christ." The true messenger of God will give all of the glory to God and boast in his own weakness and unworthiness. It was God's mercy on Paul that he was burdened with a "thorn in his flesh" so that he would never again become puffed up, for his protection. Paul went through great punishment and trial so that the strength of Christ would be made perfectly manifest in him and authenticate his message of God's love and grace.

Grace is all we need. When we hurt, let us long for grace. When we are tempted, look only toward God's grace for the ability to resist and instead do good. When we sin, it is grace that stands before us, even as the devil stands aside of us with words of guilt and shame.

Reach for God's grace; it saved you, it heals you, it has already forgiven you, and it longs to hold you in love. When we become weak, we do not fail because of it. We are forgiven sinners. Look for God's grace.

Don't deny who you are; you will fail. Be true to who you are: a sinner saved by grace. You are still a sinner and always will be.[230] You are a sinner with the living God residing on the inside of you.[231] But you also live inside of Him where there can be no sin![232] This is the nature of the power of the Blood!

Be Christ through His strength. We are sinners but do not need to sin; but if we do, we are protected in Christ.[233] Allow God to heal your heart.[234] Allow God to show you the way out of temptation.[235] He is the Way, and the way is in Him as you are in Him.

Allow God to show you how much He loves you and forgave you on the cross before you ever sinned.[236] Allow God's grace to be all you need, and you will know peace and joy in Christ. His grace is sufficient for me in my strength and in my weakness. Let it be for you too.

*God's Promise:*
God's grace is all you need. Let it flow in you, and overflow from you.

# Authority in Weakness

> For to be sure, he was crucified in weakness,
> yet he lives by God's power. Likewise, we are
> weak in him, yet by God's power we will live
> with him in our dealing with you. This is why
> I write these things when I am absent, that
> when I come I may not have to be harsh in my
> use of authority—the authority
> the Lord gave me for building you up,
> not for tearing you down.
>
> —2 Corinthians 13:4, 10 (NIV)

Paul wrote two-thirds of the New Testament by God's power and with the authority of Christ. His goal in writing was to build up the church, to lead new believers in truth, and to dispel false teachings.

His power came as a result of his weakness as he fully subjected himself as one living in and with Jesus Christ. As a result, the authority of teaching was made manifest in him with words spoken by the Holy Spirit through his heart to the churches.

We receive this same power to speak truth when we die to self and become weak in love to the cross as

Jesus did. For then as Jesus rose from the dead by the power of God, so we rise from our death to self to life in God and speak by His power according to His will.

It is for this reason I write. I write to all believers as a result of my weakness in Christ to the cross. I know I am weak, for the grace of God remains sufficient for all my needs. I boast of nothing except my desire to do the will of God in love and duty to the Gospel.

The more I ponder God's magnificence, the more I understand how pathetic I am but for the grace and miracles of life and salvation. If my thoughts were weighed before Christ, they would alone bury me, even without any actions. So I serve Him not because of my past but because of my promised future.[237]

Knowing this, test all things against two to three elder witnesses, and remember, the Word is living and perfect in truth for instruction and edification.[238] We speak only truth so that no defense is needed when we meet again, in our weakness and humility, for your strengthening in the faith.

The life subjected to Christ is granted full power in Him.[239] The Holy Spirit is the most powerful force on earth, and He lives in us. When we give Him all the credit for our words, they move about as a living force, and truth becomes our bond in the body of Christ.[240] Be humble and meek and speak life!

*God's Promise:*
Authority is ours for strengthening the body of Christ, not for judging anyone. By this intent we can discern truth speakers and life givers from the enemy.

# Faith in the Gospel

> For I am not ashamed of the gospel, because it is the power of God that brings salvation to everyone who believes: first to the Jew, then to the Gentile. For in the gospel the righteousness of God is revealed— a righteousness that is by faith from first to last, just as it is written: "The righteous will live by faith."
>
> —Romans 1:16–17 (NIV)

It is the Gospel that we live for. The Gospel has a name, and it is Jesus Christ.[241] The Gospel has a summary, and it is that those who believe in Him will be saved. The Gospel has a story, and it is the complete Holy Bible. The Gospel is man's story and how God intervened to rescue us from our depraved minds through the faith of righteousness to win victory over evil through love.

To be ashamed of the Gospel is to be ashamed of God. It is God who has saved you by the Gospel, not so that you would be jealous of the unsaved but be vibrant and bold for your Savior. The Gospel is intended to live in and through you.

Your responsibility to the Gospel is not simply to

try to convert everyone you meet, for you have no power to do this anyway; it is your changed and reborn spirit that is to preach the Gospel through your actions.[242] You are responsible for the message, not how it is received.

God imputed His righteousness to us when we were transformed into living vessels for His Holy Spirit.[243] We are the righteousness of God by the atoning work of the blood of Christ in and through us. It is by faith in the righteousness of Christ that God has entrusted us with the precious Gospel message of salvation. To be ashamed of the Gospel is to be ashamed of yourself.[244]

Christ bore all your shame on the cross, so why would you choose to allow more shame to hide the work He has done for you?[245] Be transformed in the body, mind, and spirit by the Gospel of Jesus Christ.[246]

The song of love never ends for the servant who lives out the righteousness of God in them as children of faith. We trust His Word because we have read His Word, believed His Word, walked in His Word, and seen His Word come to pass.[247] Our faith is a faith of action, not of passive hope, but of practical experience.[248]

Our salvation is one of God's faith in the power of love. The transformation of our life is to move others to want what God has done in us and for us. When others see our faith in God, and God blessing us with power and stronger faith, they are drawn to the Gospel and the love of God.

The righteous will live by faith, and all believers

are made righteous through Christ's blood.[249] There is nothing that can stain the robe washed by the blood in the righteousness of Christ.

Let our faith shine through action, for this is the key to the Gospel. We do not have the power to save, only the power to demonstrate by faith that we have been saved. It is the power of God to save all who believe.[250] First, let them believe that you are saved by faith, then they may believe that God really does save, and can also save them.

*God's Promise:*

If the Gospel is seen in you, and if others can believe it, God will bring salvation to them through your life of righteousness lived by faith in Christ.

# Righteous Judgment

> But because of your stubbornness and your unrepentant heart, you are storing up wrath against yourself for the day of God's wrath, when his righteous judgment will be revealed. God "will repay each person according to what they have done." To those who by persistence in doing good seek glory, honor and immortality, he will give eternal life. But for those who are self-seeking and who reject the truth and follow evil, there will be wrath and anger. There will be trouble and distress for every human being who does evil: first for the Jew, then for the Gentile; but glory, honor and peace for everyone who does good: first for the Jew, then for the Gentile. For God does not show favoritism. This will take place on the day when God judges people's secrets through Jesus Christ, as my gospel declares.
>
> —Romans 2:5–11, 16 (NIV)

God is not a respecter of persons. He does not compare you to another, so you cannot judge your life by what someone else does or does not do. We can only compare our lives to the standards of the Bible.

We are to love our brothers and sisters in Christ with all our heart and serve them doing good.[251] We are to love the rest of the world and serve them according to grace in love.[252]

The key to a life of rewards is love. We must love ourselves enough to forgive ourselves, for we are a forgiven people. We must love others enough to forgive them of their sins, whether they are sorry or not, for they are a forgiven people, whether they accept it or not.[253]

We must love God enough to obey His commandments and repent from our self-seeking desires and evil thoughts. We must love Jesus enough to let Him live His life through us and follow Him doing good works of mercy for the poor and lost. We must love the Holy Spirit enough to keep His temple clean and orderly, which is our reasonable duty.[254]

God is love. Be thankful He holds back His wrath and anger in mercy and love.[255] He has given us to Jesus as an inheritance and calls us to repent daily and choose to love Jesus, not self and this fallen world.[256]

If we carry the stubbornness of unrepentance to our grave, God's anger will be revealed to us on Judgment Day. We have the life of Christ inside of us, giving us the righteousness of God. We have the Spirit of God giving us the mind of Christ to know right from wrong. We have no excuse to hold on to selfish desires instead of doing God's will.

Every person will be judged according to their works, whether good or bad, of value or ashes, whether done in love or in pride. Every person will be judged according to the secrets of their heart.

Do you speak and act out of a desire to bring glory and honor to the name of Jesus Christ your Savior? Or do you find yourself speaking and acting out of a desire to guard your pride and win the praise of men? What is your motive for every thought and deed? Is it to bring honor to the God who created you, gives you life, and saved you by grace? Or is it to be comfortable in this world?

We have been immensely blessed with riches in America and are afraid to even speak the name of Jesus in the workplace for fear of judgment from man. Meanwhile, Christians are killed every single day around the world for their faith in Jesus.[257] God does not show favoritism, so what are you doing to bring glory and honor to your Savior, Lord, and King?

*God's Promise:*
The believer will be judged by the secrets of the heart according to the love they have shown, even the love they have desired to show.

# Righteousness by Faith

> But now apart from the law the righteousness of God has been made known, to which the Law and the Prophets testify. This righteousness is given through faith in Jesus Christ to all who believe. There is no difference between Jew and Gentile, for all have sinned and fall short of the glory of God, and all are justified freely by his grace through the redemption that came by Christ Jesus.
>
> —Romans 3:21–24 (NIV)

Faith makes us worthy of eternal life with our Holy Father. We read and hear about this Jesus, and we feel the tug of our heart that He loves us. We either ignore it or search it out by looking through our mind's eye to reason it possible that we could be loved by a perfect Creator.

Then the mystery of faith is revealed to us. At some moment in time, the necessary measure of faith is handed to each one of us in due part, unique to everyone: the "to be saved" and the "to be lost," and we choose our destiny. If God sees our heart believe in the love of Christ that forgives our sins, we are given His righteousness and saved.[258] If we deny we sin or see Christ as unneeded, unable, or unwilling, we remain lost.

Faith in the love of Christ to bear our sin-debt makes us righteous in Him. He suffered on our behalf, the just for the unjust, to allow us to be free.[259]

This measured out faith never ends, for we are justified freely by God, not that any of us can boast, for no one does good, and all our fleshy ways are rubbish before Holy God. Our nature is corrupt, and unless God gives us a new nature, His holiness, we can do no good.[260] Accept it. This is why God hates pride so much, because we are all the same sinful men with the same beginning, same end, and same fruitless existence without eternal value unless He saves us from our fate.[261]

We have no right to judge anyone, for our righteousness as children of God is not our own—it is Christ's righteousness. So understand that any good we can do, even observing the law or Jesus's commands, is through Christ's goodness, not our own.

It is by faith that we are saved, but this faith is not of our own but of God; fortunately, we chose to use it to call to God for mercy, because at that moment, we saw our sinfulness and repented.

*God's Promise:*
The believer is not better than anyone, only better off by the grace of God.

# The Promise

> Therefore, the promise comes by faith, so that it may be by grace and may be guaranteed to all Abraham's offspring—not only to those who are of the law but also to those who have the faith of Abraham. He is the father of us all. As it is written: "I have made you a father of many nations." He is our father in the sight of God, in whom he believed—the God who gives life to the dead and calls into being things that were not.
>
> —Romans 4:16–17 (NIV)

Only by faith can we receive the kingdom of God. We are all unworthy of God's kingdom, whether we call ourselves righteous or intentionally do wrong.[262]

God calls forth the dead into life.[263] It is by His grace that life ever existed. It is by His grace that life is given back to those who have died. We are all spiritually dead because of sin and, therefore, can do nothing to become alive again on our own. We can only trust in the Giver of life to have mercy on us. Only by seeing ourselves as helpless before our Holy Father can we have faith in Jesus Christ.

This is what makes religion so dangerous. There are so many "Christians" who have been raised in religious denominational churches where being good is thought to credit them with righteousness. They believe they are going to heaven because they go to church, wear head coverings, don't play cards, don't play outside on Sunday, etc. Not everyone who practices these things does them for the wrong reasons. You will know them by their works, whether good works of love to show Christ living in them, or by works of the law.[264]

The law was given so we would know sin and understand our need for a savior.[265] It is only by faith that we can receive the kingdom of God, which is the promise to be returned to God, and to be with God, as we originally were: created in His image.[266]

It was grace that gave Adam breath; it was grace that gave Abraham righteousness; it was grace that raised Lazarus from the dead; it was grace that brought forth Jesus from the dead to walk amongst the disciples; it was grace that brought forth the baptism with the Holy Spirit so we could be given life in the righteousness of Christ through faith in God.

We are all the same in Christ: sinners saved by grace and grace alone! We are all one in Him!

*God's Promise:*
It is only by God's grace through faith you have been called from spiritual death into life eternal as heirs of the promise.

# Peace and Hope

Therefore, since we have been justified
through faith, we have peace with God
through our Lord Jesus Christ,
through whom we have gained access
by faith into this grace in which we now
stand. And we boast in the hope
of the glory of God. Not only so,
but we also glory in our sufferings,
because we know that
suffering produces perseverance;
perseverance, character;
and character, hope.
And hope does not put us to shame,
because God's love has been poured out
into our hearts through the Holy Spirit,
who has been given to us.

—Romans 5:1–5 (NIV)

How can a man threatened with torture and the murder of his family stand before his accusers and not deny Jesus Christ as Lord and very God? It is because of the hope placed within our hearts by the outpouring of God's love through the Holy Spirit, gifted to us all who have faith in the blood of Jesus.

We all have peace with God, having been justified by Jesus Christ. God no longer sees our sin when He looks at us; He only sees Jesus.[267]

Jesus is always interceding for us with God so that only love and grace would emanate from heaven, through Christ, into our hearts and lives by the presence of the Holy Spirit living inside of us.[268]

God has invested all He has and had to offer through His sacrificial death on a criminal's tree in order to give us peace and hope, even though we deserve only death.[269]

We have been given by grace faith in Jesus Christ, the hope of glory.

We long for our glorified bodies so that we may be present before our glorified Savior and found in the eternal glory of God.[270]

Therefore, the Holy Spirit seals this glory in us by a continual outpouring of grace directly from the glory of God so that by faith, we may have the hope of the greater glory, which does await us. We long then, as the Spirit testifies in us, for our glorified body, the perfect temple for communion with God.[271]

Because of the peace and hope we have been given through grace, we persevere by faith and build the character of Jesus Christ, which is our perfect end through sanctification.

Our new man nature longs to share in the sufferings of Christ who suffered willingly for us while we were still enemies of Him.[272]

We hope not only for glory to come, but for glory already revealed in us by the love of God the Holy Spirit.

*God's Promise:*

God gave us the Comforter to seal our salvation, sanctify us, and give us the hope of His glory and glory to come.

# All

> Consequently, just as one trespass resulted in condemnation for all people, so also one righteous act resulted in justification and life for all people. For just as through the disobedience of the one man the many were made sinners, so also through the obedience of the one man the many will be made righteous.
>
> —Romans 5:18–19 (NIV)

Man's spirit died because of sin. By Adam's sin, his spirit died. Because his spirit died, he lost his holy nature and developed the sinful nature now known as human nature. Because he was now simply human, he could not pass on a holy nature to his children; instead, he passed on his sinful nature. And because we live in a cursed land full of thorns and snares, this sinful nature produces the fruit of its tree: sin. And the wages of sin is death.[273]

Death comes because of sin. Any child who lives long enough to make conscious decisions eventually chooses to do what is contrary to that which is good and acceptable and sins against the righteousness of God. Because of Adam, all men die.[274]

Whether in the womb because of the mother's sin, or in this world because of our own sin, we all must die. Once the child chooses to disobey, the mother's own sin looses hold on the eventual cause of death for the child, and the child has now become responsible for his or her own sentence to death. This new death sentence comes with eternal consequences, however, added unto the physical death sentence from the mother's sinful nature passing on to the growing child. Now, because the child has consciously determined to do what is wrong, knowing instead what was right, because the law of the parents was right and just in the eyes of God, sin has come into its full measure, and eternal separation from God is the natural result.[275]

The man who sins separates himself from that which is holy by free will.[276] He can no longer do eternally good things because his spirit has died. The mother held natural death over the child as a result of her sinful nature, but once the child sins, like Adam, his spirit dies, and physical death is joined with spiritual death. Where the spirit is dead, God cannot join men with His holy presence, for darkness and light do not mix. They are stark opposites. The light must always consume the darkness.[277]

The gift of life is the gift of the holy presence of God.[278] God breathes life into a child.[279] Without the Spirit of God, there is no life.

God cannot breathe life and death into a child at the same time. Death comes by sin, personal sin, personal disobedience, and personal choices.

The life of the child is flesh built up from the dust of the mother and father by the Great Builder; it is a soul created in heaven by mystery; it is a spirit of life and breath originating from the mouth of God the Holy Spirit.

God gives life, not death. A child is born with a spirit of life, trapped within a sinful flesh. The body screams out: angered by the living spirit within it which draws unto God; wanting its own desires fulfilled which are contrary to the fruit of the Spirit.[280]

The battle between flesh and spirit is on, and it is fueled by the sinful world into which the child is born. Death, pain, and all sorts of struggle surround the new child, thwarting even a righteous mother's attempts to provide a safe environment for rearing.[281]

Sin creeps in—to some early, to others late.[282] But for any child who lives long enough to make a conscious choice, the human nature takes over, and the choice to disobey comes naturally, as does the consequence: spiritual death.

Enter the Savior of the world! Our hopeless condition has been heard. Our time of futility is ended. A Savior has come to break the chains of death.[283] The grip of sinful nature has been released. The Spirit of righteousness and life has returned to all mankind. Christ has broken the chain. All men can now have life again in Him. He died for us all![284] Adam's curse is over for those who believe in Jesus.[285] Praise the Lord! Praise His precious name! Hallelujah!

*God's Promise:*
The Holy Spirit gave us life, but we chose death; but we can choose life again through Jesus Christ.

# Dead to Sin

We were therefore buried with him through baptism into death in order that, just as Christ was raised from the dead through the glory of the Father, we too may live a new life. For we know that our old self was crucified with him so that the body ruled by sin might be done away with, that we should no longer be slaves to sin—
In the same way, count yourselves dead to sin but alive to God in Christ Jesus. For sin shall no longer be your master, because you are not under the law, but under grace. You have been set free from sin and have become slaves to righteousness.

—Romans 6:4, 6, 11, 14, 18 (NIV)

There are no longer any rules to follow. We have been set free from sin. We are no longer under the law; we are under God's grace. It is for freedom that Christ set us free. And those Christ sets free are free indeed!

To sin is to know what is the right thing to do but to choose not to do it.[286] It is as simple as knowing that you should say, "I was wrong," but choosing not to apologize. Sin is as simple as knowing to drive the speed limit but choosing instead, for no reason except your own desire or lack of self-control, to go faster. Sin is as simple as knowing you should go see your mother but instead choosing to go golfing.

In a nutshell, we sin every day by knowing what we ought to do but excusing ourselves to do otherwise. God has placed in the heart of the believer His Holy Spirit to speak to our conscience and guide us in truth. We are of no excuse, but also of helpless condition.

Enter the Savior. He lived a perfect and holy life, always doing what was right according to the guidance of the Holy Spirit revealing God's will. He accomplished the Father's will by allowing us to crucify Him. As a perfect sacrifice, God placed the sin of the world into the body of Christ and crucified Him on a criminal's cross.[287]

Murdered as a sinner, the Christ became sin, and God buried Him, with all the sin-guilt of the world, into the tomb. Dead, Christ carried our sins down into Hades and cast them before the devil into the lake of fire, never again to be remembered by God or held against us by God or the law.[288]

Finished, God called forth His Son back to life. Sin was defeated! We were set free![289]

But we did not know it.

Enter the Holy Spirit. What Jesus did was obviously supernatural and extraordinary. By no words could we grasp what Jesus did for us. No unbeliever can read Romans Chapter 6 and even grasp the concept.[290]

Knowing that even the love Jesus was not enough to change us while in this world, God had to baptize us with His holy presence into the body of Christ. This was accomplished by the person of the Holy Spirit.[291] He superimposes upon us the eternal benefits of what Jesus did on the cross now, while yet in these bodies.[292] Jesus was enough to get us to heaven, but the Holy Spirit was needed to have enough power to live victoriously on earth and serve God in love.

The Holy Spirit baptized us into Christ's death on the cross and into the grave. Our physical bodies, by divine substitution, were crucified and buried dead as part of the eternal body of Christ. By divine substitution, our spirit was born again by the power of the Holy Spirit. Our physical body was purchased with the price of the blood of God so that now we are made alive in Christ![293]

Very simply put, we are dead to sin because sin has no power over Christ! Sin has no power over us unless we choose to give it power. We are free in Christ!

The devil has been defeated. The grave has been defeated. Sin has been defeated. Our sinful nature has been defeated. We have been crucified with Christ!

Our past, present, and future sin has been cast into the lake of fire, and because light and darkness cannot coexist, God not only chooses not to see our sin, but He cannot see it; He chose to cast it away from His presence forever! Christ became our sin—He died and buried it forever. By the power of the Holy Spirit, He returned to the Father glorified and holy with us: His restored body, His eternal church, His perfect bride.

We are now slaves to God, purified by the blood of Christ and sanctified by the Holy Spirit.[294] What is left is up to us. We can seek the truth and feed our spirit or choose to disobey the Spirit and serve our flesh.[295]

It is not sin that we serve but either God or self. Yet grace abounds to all because of Christ. We either choose eternal rewards and blessings for serving Jesus in love, or we choose temporal rewards by serving ourselves in disobedience.

Choose eternity and shed the chains. We are free to love. The power of sin has been defeated.

*God's Promise:*
Those who Christ has set free are free indeed. We are truly free in Christ!

# Dead to the Law

> So, my brothers and sisters, you also died to the law through the body of Christ, that you might belong to another, to him who was raised from the dead, in order that we might bear fruit for God. For when we were in the realm of the flesh, the sinful passions aroused by the law were at work in us, so that we bore fruit for death. But now, by dying to what once bound us, we have been released from the law so that we serve in the new way of the Spirit, and not in the old way of the written code.
>
> —Romans 7:4–6 (NIV)

The law of God made sin be known. The law was intended to give life, but man found that it only brought death, for the law is perfect, and man is imperfect.

Jesus became the propitiation for our sins and died a criminal's death as if a sinner, but He was indeed perfect and sinless. Since God is just, Christ's death must also have been just. The Holy Spirit took us from the clutches of death's grasp, while we yet held breath of life, and placed us spiritually on the cross with Jesus. Our death, due to our inability to keep the whole law, was imparted into the body of Christ, who perfectly fulfilled the whole law.[296] For this He was crucified and buried dead for three days.[297] Since Jesus willingly took upon Himself our sin-guilt and death sentence, His death became just in the eyes of God.

Our death, both spiritual and physical, was trumped by Christ's resurrection, and we were given eternal life by the imputation of Christ's righteousness.[298] This too was a work of the Holy Spirit, directed by grace with authorization made by the Lawmaker Himself, such that a new law presides over the hearts of men—the law of grace! The law of deeds is dead.

Now baptized into the eternal body of Christ, there is no escape.[299] We have died to the law, been resurrected, and given eternal life in Christ. Only if God the Father Himself could die could we leave this new life![300]

We have been given life for a single reason—to bear fruit for God![301] We are saved to do good works! We no longer serve the law of sin and death but serve the living God and the law of grace! We are free in Christ to love each other! We have been saved to serve our Father for His glory!

The law no longer has power over us. But we cherish the law, for by it, we know what is good and pleasing to God. The difference is that the law has a new administrator—the Holy Spirit.[302] The old law was administered by sinful man, and no one could keep it. Now the living Spirit convicts us of right and wrong and does not condemn but administers grace according to what is profitable for us to have a sanctifying relationship with God through the intercession provided by Jesus Christ.

We have been freed from the law so that we may serve the Lord by working with the Holy Spirit. The Holy Spirit's work is to make the Gospel known, to make the Word of God effective unto salvation, and to convict men to repent and react to the call of God. The Holy Spirit guides the believer in righteousness to know the mind of God for each one's life in His perfect and unique will.

There is no longer a universal law for everyone except the law of grace, which is love. God loves His children. He is the Administrator of gentle grace to each one of us. His will is designed perfectly for each one of us. If His grace is sufficient for anyone, it is sufficient for you and certainly for me.[303]

We are dead to the law of sin and death and made eternally alive in Christ so that we may serve Him in love by grace.

*God's Promise:*
We have been set free from the law but only so that we may serve our God in spirit and in truth.

# Two Masters

> So I find this law at work: Although I want to do good, evil is right there with me. For in my inner being I delight in God's law; but I see another law at work in me, waging war against the law of my mind and making me a prisoner of the law of sin at work within me. What a wretched man I am! Who will rescue me from this body that is subject to death? Thanks be to God, who delivers me through Jesus Christ our Lord! So then, I myself in my mind am a slave to God's law, but in my sinful nature a slave to the law of sin.
>
> —Romans 7:21–25 (NIV)

Before we were saved, we served the devil, for we were at enmity with God because of our inability to keep His commandments. Oh, there were some who did some good but only by God's special favor and Holy Spirit's protection in order to serve God's divine purpose. But they too fell and recognized even the more their own sin and unworthiness.

Men only ever served God in fear because the Holy Spirit placed their heart before a holy mirror. Now, we love the law, for by it we see God's goodness and holiness, for the holy mirror is no longer in front of us but inside of us!

Two laws are in us now, and we serve two masters. We are finally slaves to righteousness, but at the same time remain slaves to sin. We are a slave to the One because of Christ's atoning blood and the Holy Spirit living inside of us, but we are also a slave to the other because we are still trapped in a sinful body—a corrupted flesh with a rebellious nature.

The change has brought with it a true love for God, which before could not be grasped. We now serve God because we love Him and His law! We delight in His law because it shows us how to please Him. God is pleased when we repent from sin, not necessarily when we remain sinless.[304]

God is just and delights in the repentant and humble heart, for He knows our sinful condition. Jesus lived trapped in human flesh, walking with sinners, for thirty-three years. He knows what it is like to be trapped in the flesh yet deeply loving the Father with all your heart. He knows the struggles we face.

Jesus was unable to serve the master of the flesh, however, because flesh was created for and by Him; by nature, Jesus is the Master of the flesh and, therefore, wielded mastery over sin and the body's sinful nature.[305] So too we can have mastery over the sinful nature of our flesh through Christ in us.

We delight in the law because it guides us in pleasing God and teaches us to be more like Christ.[306] This is a sanctifying process though, only to be completed when our flesh dies and we are given our new eternal bodies. Since we did not create flesh, we remain a slave to its nature. The flesh has been perfecting its sinful nature for at least six thousand years! The fact that we can overcome any part of its power is only a testament to the power of Christ in us, the hope of glory.[307]

So we now have two masters but have the freedom to love the One and hate the other. Followers of Christ no longer love their sin but hate it, for the love of God has taken sin's place by the new law of mercy and grace. We must choose whom we will love, and whom we will serve. This is the gift of free will, and the administration of the law of grace.

*God's Promise:*
The born-again believer has two masters: the flesh and the Spirit. We serve both as slaves but through Christ can choose to only love the One.

# Free in Christ

> Therefore, there is now no condemnation for those who are in Christ Jesus, because through Christ Jesus the law of the Spirit who gives life has set you free from the law of sin and death.
>
> —Romans 8:1–2 (NIV)

What does it mean to be free? Here in America we boast about freedom, but we are not truly free. We can no longer pray in schools or even voice our faith in Christ without the world attacking us for offending someone. And that is outside the law!

We are bound by more laws in this country than any one person is even aware of. Unless you stay in bed all day and are caught up on all your bills, you will probably break a common law or offend some civil liberty. And let's face it, can anyone say they have not exceeded the speed limit or rolled through a stop sign?

We are certainly not free in the physical sense, nor should we be. So what does freedom in Christ mean?

We need to understand first what is the law of sin. By Adam's disobedience, sin came to all mankind. Adam had perfect flesh. His body was designed to live forever. But sin caused him to die because that was God's law.[308]

Adam's death came by sin and was passed on to all of us. Very simple. But what this means to us is that we cannot avoid sin, because sin is to know what is right and to do otherwise.[309]

The law of sin and death is established by the struggles of Israel throughout the Old Testament. Man cannot do good on his own.[310] Man's best attempt at being righteous killed the Son of God.[311] The law of sin is that none do good; no, not one, and as a result, all die.[312]

But God, by His perfect and unending mercy, came to save us. We are not released from sin and death, but we are released from the law that binds us to it in chains. We are not free from sin: we are free from the law, which requires a payment for it. We are not free from death: we are free from the law that makes it a permanent separation from God.

Next, we need to understand what the law of the Spirit is. The law of the Spirit is grace.

Say it with me: "God's grace is sufficient for me." Don't ever forget this. It is the substance of life: grace.

God's grace imagined you, then created you, loved you, and saved you. Now God's grace sustains you!

It is grace that says, "There is nothing you can do to make me love you less than the day I created you or the day I saved you."

Grace. Grace. It is all about grace. God loves us so fully that He wants nothing more than for us to grow to be like Him, and He will make us like Him by His grace.[313]

We deserve nothing; grace gives us everything. The law of the Spirit is grace.[314] Grace covers all our sins such that we can never sin enough to cause God to leave us![315] We are covered like a dead leaf under a blanket of snow by the righteousness of Christ. God's perfection has been given to us by grace.[316] We are perfect in God's eyes because Jesus was perfect![317] Grace on grace with grace!

Who Christ has set free on Calvary by paying their debt and defeating the grave is free indeed! We cannot promise God anything except to love Him, praise Him, and follow Jesus. Being free, we must accept that all that comes our way only makes us more like Christ through spiritual growth. We must realize that we are appointed to good works but only as we follow Jesus Christ.[318]

We cannot do good works on our own. We cannot dive into the world for Jesus and expect Him to "have our back." We are who we are because that is who God has made us to be in the body of Christ.[319] If we are sick, it is to demonstrate His faith and healing. If we are drunk, it is to show His grace and to humble us. If we are a fool, it is for Christ we stumble and fall. We are only here to do God's will, and we are free to do it, in Christ, for Christ, and by Christ.[320]

We cannot successfully be greater than God's will for our lives. He has a divine will for our lives, and we must accept His grace to sustain us in our sinful and human nature to accomplish His will.[321]

Christ died to set us free, not make us perfect humans. He set us free from the law, not free from the flesh. Our spirit is now perfect and also perfectly opposed to our flesh. Jesus rose from the grave to give us life in Him, not life in front of Him.

Do not fall prey to works for acceptance. Do good works because it is in His common will and within His purposeful will for your life. Pray that each and every good work is done by following Him to where He is already at work.

His grace is sufficient for you. You are free in Christ. Everything is yours.[322] Choose to be everything He has anointed you to be but nothing He has not designed you to be; choose to be loved and sustained by grace. In love, through His grace, you will find complete victory over your flesh, the devil, and the wiles of this world.

*God's Promise:*

We are free in Christ to love the ones Jesus died to save because He first loved us with His own life.

# Help Is Here

> In the same way, the Spirit helps us in our weakness. We do not know what we ought to pray for, but the Spirit himself intercedes for us through wordless groans. And he who searches our hearts knows the mind of the Spirit, because the Spirit intercedes for God's people in accordance with the will of God.
>
> —Romans 8:26–27 (NIV)

We have proven ourselves a helpless people. This is why Jesus sent us a helper. We must ask for His help, and He will help.[323]

In our sinful condition, the mind does not know how to be free from the control of the flesh because it is trapped in it. But the Spirit of God somehow mysteriously lives in us and gives our spirit new life in Him. The Holy Spirit knows our minds and gives us perfect access to the Father, who knows both our hearts and the mind of His Spirit.

This is how it works. We must give up our striving and yield to the direction of the Spirit. In humility, we call to the Holy Spirit to help when we do not know how to help ourselves. When we are at a place where we recognize that we cannot escape the lust of the flesh on our own, we are in a good place to be. Only the Holy Spirit can assure we are at peace with God and walking within the will of God.

Our flesh is no stronger now than when we were first saved. It is our spirit that gets stronger in Christ by the resurrection power of His Holy Spirit.

Christ did not save us to be sinless. He saved us to forgive our past, present, and future sins so that we could have hope in Him. We are free from the power of our sin.

So sin remains as long as we are trapped in this flesh. Whereas before God had to punish sin, atone for sin, or turn His back on sin, it is now used by God to grow us spiritually to be more and more like Christ until the day we are freed from these bodies.

The miracle of the cross is that sin was made powerless. Christ triumphed over the law of sin and death and made us free and slaves to His righteousness. In this miraculous grace, our shortcomings no longer keep us from the presence of God. Instead, in our weakness we become stronger!

Sanctification unto holiness is a lifelong process.[324] We must forgive ourselves, for we have been forgiven. It is the will of God to make you holy and into the image of Christ, but this is not a goal realized fully until we die. This whole life experience is to teach us about holiness and the failure of worldliness. Life teaches us that all of God's ways are good and that none of our ways are.

When we feel hopeless to do good, we yield to the Spirit and God's will. The Holy Spirit speaks directly to the Father on our behalf. We know that all of our experiences are within His permissive will to make us holy. He gently teaches us about His enduring love and faithfulness. He demonstrates to the world through us the perfection of His peace and grace. All this is made manifest in us by the eternally atoning work of the blood of Jesus Christ.

*God's Promise:*
We have the Holy Spirit to plead on our behalf to God our Father, who knows our hearts and flesh better than we do because of Christ in us; and we always have a Helper in time of need to comfort us with peace in God's perfect will.

# God's Purpose

> And we know that in all things God works
> for the good of those who love him, who
> have been called according to his purpose.
> For those God foreknew he also predestined
> to be conformed to the image of his Son,
> that he might be the firstborn among
> many brothers and sisters.
> And those he predestined, he also called;
> those he called, he also justified;
> those he justified, he also glorified.
>
> —Romans 8:28–30 (NIV)

The extraordinary life begins when you accept who you are in Christ. Know your worth to God.

We were created by God in His image in heaven long before we were born.[325] Our soul was sent to earth to accomplish God's purpose (also known as His divine will) for our lives. Our soul has always been sustained by His Spirit so that we can commune with Him and be in His presence.

Our spirit died when we sinned. We quickly forgot about where we came from and how to get back there. Many of us forgot that we needed God for anything. But this death left a void which God used to call us back home. It left a void only perfect love could fill, and this perfect love was made manifest in Jesus Christ.

God's purpose is to make us like the resurrected and glorified Jesus. Jesus painfully experienced the consequences of our sins on the cross. He underwent a conscious suffering of what it was like to be separated from God.[326] We will not suffer for our sins like Jesus did. Neither will we have to know what separation from our God was actually like due to the gift of intentional forgetfulness.

God's purpose is to make us like Christ. He uses everything that happens to us to accomplish this goal: good and bad, sin and suffering, mercy and grace. Nothing is wasted in the economy of God. All things work for good to those chosen in Him. We are here to accomplish His will, and He is faithful to do it. Jesus came to fully understand our freedom to love or hate, to experience our fallen condition, and to teach us how to choose life and the goodness of God.[327]

Our resurrected purpose is to become perfect like Jesus through our experiences here on earth and to do the same works of love that Jesus did. Be like Christ and do what Christ did because that is God's purpose for your life.[328] We know that everything makes us more like Him because God will use it, whether good or bad, to grow us spiritually.

Life is not a mystery for the Christian. It is completely revealed to us here in these three verses by Paul. We were with God in eternity and sent to earth to fulfill our individual calling as well as our collective calling. We are all saved to be made like the man Jesus Christ. We have been predestined to be made like God's perfect Son that when we die, we will be raised from the dead and given glorified bodies, like Jesus, so that we are called His brothers and sisters.

The purpose of life is therefore to be like Christ. This is not a passive purpose but a lifelong and active process. This is why God promises us that He works all things for the good of attaining this purpose.

We must fully seek to be like Jesus by exercising our faith and new spirit of life doing good works of love and mercy. If God works our bad deeds for good according to His purpose of making us like Jesus, imagine how glorious He will work our deeds of love for Jesus and our fellow man.

*God's Promise:*

God knew us before we were born, sent us to earth according to His purpose, called us to be saved, then justified us and glorified us in Christ Jesus as joint heirs of His eternal kingdom.

# The Love of God

> Who shall separate us from the love of Christ? Shall trouble or hardship or persecution or famine or nakedness or danger or sword? No, in all these things we are more than conquerors through him who loved us. For I am convinced that neither death nor life, neither angels nor demons, neither the present nor the future, nor any powers, neither height nor depth, nor anything else in all creation, will be able to separate us from the love of God that is in Christ Jesus our Lord.
>
> —Romans 8:35, 37–39 (NIV)

Nothing and no one separates us from the love of God. These are the most comforting words ever spoken to a Christian found in Christ Jesus. Once saved by the blood, always saved. God is not God if we could sin enough to get unsaved and out from under His covenant of blood. When Jesus said, "It is finished," He meant it.[329]

All sin is covered by His blood. All of the devil's power over us has been defeated. The Holy Spirit enters a man upon salvation and will never leave us.[330]

So what then do we say to this, the ultimate

promise? We say that we are free in Christ! We are guaranteed saved, sealed, and delivered into the loving arms of God for eternity![331] We are loved perfectly and forever.

Nothing can ever change God's full and perfect love for us. We can do no wrong in His eyes, for even the worst we can do will only aid in perfecting us. God only sees us through the blood washed veil of Christ's righteousness. We are left to freely follow Jesus and love ourselves, all of mankind, and our God.

We are free to love and serve our Lord. This is our command: to serve others in love. The God who saved us now lives in us to make this possible and desirable.[332] The purpose of the Holy Spirit in us is to point us to the Word and accomplish God's will in our lives. The Holy Spirit is the power of the kingdom of God.

The God of the universe now lives in us eternally! We are the most powerful forces in the spirit world, for the Holy Spirit of God lives inside of us! We can heal the sick and free the slave by a single word or an intentional touch, for we are vessels of His power and purpose. We have all been called to follow Jesus. This is why we have been saved: to be world changers.

There is a cost associated with following the ways of this world and selfish desires. Eternal rewards are handed out to the good and faithful servant. We have all been set free by the power of the cross and the glory of the risen Lord so that no one has an excuse not to fulfill God's purpose for sending you here. Do not measure your Christian life by what others have been called to do, but by the measure of love for others that is in your heart.

For example, your entire divine purpose here may have been to be saved just to share your story with a hospice nurse before you died, so that she would be saved to then save many others. You may, by this act of love, have perfectly fulfilled your entire purpose. In so doing, you will share in the eternal rewards of all those saved down the line through that nurse. Don't ever miss an opportunity to show others the love of Christ!

We all have a divine purpose for being here and being reborn in Christ, but none of us have the exact same purpose. We have been placed here in this time and place with the others around us by His purpose. The love of Christ is to be shared with all of those called to be saved as well as all of those who are perishing, for God loves all of mankind and does not desire that anyone would choose death over life.[333]

You are eternally loved and protected by God through the seal of the Holy Spirit and commanded to follow Jesus in love. Fulfill your call to live an extraordinary life by faith in the promises of God available for those who truly believe.

*God's Promise:*

We are in the presence of the love of God through faith in Jesus Christ and the eternal indwelling presence of the Holy Spirit to comfort us as we do God's work.

# Who Are You?

> What if God, although choosing to show his wrath and make his power known, bore with great patience the objects of his wrath—prepared for destruction? What if he did this to make the riches of his glory known to the objects of his mercy, whom he prepared in advance for glory—even us, whom he also called, not only from the Jews but also from the Gentiles?
>
> —Romans 9:22–24 (NIV)

Unless God had left some to be saved, even a remnant, all would have perished because of sin. Who are you to say that you are better than someone else? Yes, we are better off for sure but not better.

Knowing that God chose to save me, but not the man next to me, to show the world the great mercy that was extended when He chose to save me, must drive me to my knees in total humility and submission.[334]

The realization that all deserve death and none life, that I deserve nothing but was gifted everything by the Creator's sovereign will, must humble me to serve Him with every fiber of my body and soul.[335]

What is the pot to complain to the potter?[336] Who is man to question God?[337] Who am I that God should have saved me?[338]

I am nothing but made second to One and made like Christ for an amazing purpose: to demonstrate this amazing love to the rest of the world; to show mercy because I was shown mercy; to show grace because I live in grace; to speak peace because by Christ's sacrifice, I am at peace with God.[339]

God is not a respecter of persons. He made me, and for whatever reason, He decided to save me so His Son would have an inheritance to share His kingdom with.[340] This must drive me to my knees once again and dedicate my whole life to serving Jesus in love. I must tell the world about God's great love, that He lets any of us live in His grace. His favor on me must be shared. I must give my life away to a world in need of love. It is for this any of us were saved at all.

Who are you to choose pride and selfishness and flaunt your salvation before anyone? Let your life be a living sacrifice of love for the God who mercifully saved you.[341]

*God's Promise:*
Your salvation was a gift of mercy, proven by the lives of all those who have not received the gift.

# Discipleship

> For there is no difference between Jew and Gentile—the same Lord is Lord of all and richly blesses all who call on him, for, "Everyone who calls on the name of the Lord will be saved." How, then, can they call on the one they have not believed in? And how can they believe in the one of whom they have not heard? And how can they hear without someone preaching to them? And how can anyone preach unless they are sent? As it is written: "How beautiful are the feet of those who bring good news!"
>
> —Romans 10:12–15 (NIV)

Those who call on the name of Jesus shall be saved and richly blessed. Our desire must be to bring the good news to all the world so that others can share in the rich blessings of salvation. This must come from a love for our brothers and sisters who are not yet saved.

How can we love the unsaved if we do not love the saved?[342] If we reject the fellowship that comes from our family in Christ, brothers and sisters in the unity, we will fail our purpose of loving the unsaved with the good news of salvation. We will miss out on our blessing of sharing in God's work of bringing salvation to mankind.

How blessed are those in the sight of the Lord who excitedly bring the good news to the ones Christ died to save! We must share the Gospel because of the blessings of salvation, and we must make disciples who will share the good news because of the blessings of being a Gospel bearer!

Every believer is commanded to be a disciple, and every disciple is commanded to share the good news and then disciple those who respond to the call of salvation.[343] Those who are left at "being saved" and are not "being discipled" are left like sheep to the slaughter.[344] But those who are discipled into followers of Jesus Christ bear the good news and become reproducing trees of life and beauty.[345]

We must first be disciples and desire to be discipled before we can successfully disciple someone else. How can we share something we do not ourselves possess? Disciples successfully share the good news because the unsaved see with their own eyes the beautiful transformation of life that comes with following Jesus, and they desire it too. Be a disciple and preach the good news. Send a believer out with knowledge and wisdom to preach the Gospel as a strong and mature follower of Jesus, and you shall be called blessed.

*God's Promise:*
The Gospel comes to save those hearing what has been preached by obedient followers of Jesus.

# To Know God's Will

> Therefore, I urge you, brothers and sisters, in view of God's mercy, to offer your bodies as a living sacrifice, holy and pleasing to God—this is your true and proper worship. Do not conform to the pattern of this world, but be transformed by the renewing of your mind. Then you will be able to test and approve what God's will is—his good, pleasing and perfect will.
>
> —Romans 12:1–2 (NIV)

Sin first occurs in the mind; the body simply acts out its desires. When we see what we want with our eyes, our mind begins to devise ways in which to enjoy it, whether within the mind alone or by scheming to justify acting on the desire with our bodies. Brethren, this is anything that conforms to the ways of the world instead of the will of God.[346] We must take captive every thought to the mind of Christ and subject it to the Spirit of Christ the test of the will of God.[347]

Renew your mind daily through self-examination, prayer, repentance, and study in God's Word. The object of our worship is to glorify God with our daily lives because of the gift of His indwelling Holy Spirit who speaks to our hearts. Our minds must be purified with thoughts of Christ and God's goodness and mercy; with a fresh view of grace, we become sensitive to the voice of the Savior within us. We will be reminded that have been saved to serve God and specifically created to do His purpose here in our appointed time.

Conformance to the world cannot be boxed up and thrown away. It is a constant temptation presented to each of us such that we would choose to serve self instead of God. It is subtle, and just as Eve justified herself, and Adam himself, for partaking of the fruit, we justify our worldly bellies, even with claim that God wants us to be richly blessed and happy!

God wants us to have everything we need to fully serve Him according to His divine will for our lives, in Jesus's name![348] I cannot tell anyone what God's specific will is for them other than to spread the Gospel and make disciples with their full being through faithful sacrifice and trusting submission.

Wasting thousands of dollars on clothing, cars, vacations, and luxurious dinners does not qualify as God's perfect will when He has called us to feed the poor, comfort the sick, and tend to the needs of the widows, I assure you. Spending all your free time golfing or drinking also does not align with God's will. Sitting for hours watching the world's television, reading the gossip of Hollywood, being consumed with your favorite sports teams, and reading books with no godly purpose does not qualify as submitting your mind to the will of God.

God created you for a specific service for His Son and His kingdom that only you can fulfill. Our purpose is to seek His will for our lives in service to the One who saved us.[349]

We are to worship God with our whole life. He gave us life and gifted us eternal life so that we would fulfill our appointed tasks within the body of Christ. It is therefore our reasonable duty to take our mind captive to the knowledge that God so much desires to give us about His perfect and good will for us.

We find our divine purpose by dying to our selfish desires, for the things of this world are perishing. We accomplish our purpose by focusing our minds, with bended knees and undivided hearts, on the things of God.

*God's Promise:*

To know God's perfect will, we must forsake the desires of this world and seek His face.

# Humble Service

> For by the grace given me I say to every one of you: Do not think of yourself more highly than you ought, but rather think of yourself with sober judgment, in accordance with the faith God has distributed to each of you. For just as each of us has one body with many members, and these members do not all have the same function, so in Christ we, though many, form one body, and each member belongs to all the others.
>
> —Romans 12:3–5 (NIV)

We have all been bought with a price, the most valuable and expensive purchase ever made. God's own blood was spilled out upon this earth to purchase our lives from it.[350] The highest price possible was paid for each of our souls. Being purchased, therefore, by God, we became owned by Him and were gifted back to Jesus Christ, who Himself was the money paid.

God's reward to Jesus for His sacrifice is the Church, and Jesus in turn shares His precious gifts with each of us. We no longer belong to ourselves, our sinful and selfish selves, but we belong to Christ, and in Christ, we belong to each other—to every Christian in the world we belong individually and collectively.

God's gifts to us, both the spiritual gifts as well as the tangible gifts of this world, were given to us to serve Him and His body of believers. Everything we have—our talents, skills, heart, home, career, and money—were given to us solely to be used to serve others.

How dare we believe that God blessed us in our wealth because He thinks we are better than the poor and persecuted Christian in Sudan, Syria, or Iraq who has nothing but the little breath he has left to praise God for His grace before he is murdered for his faith. We may not think we believe this is so, but if we examine our lives to see if they speak to self-entitlement or sacrificial giving to the body of Christ, especially the persecuted church, we may be surprised by the truth.

We are called to be good stewards of what God has given to us. We may think we earned our gifts, or even deserve them, but we deserve only death for our sin. But God, in His infinite mercy and grace, gave us life eternal and blessings of favor that we would love Him and, in turn, take all that we have been given and sacrificially give it back to those in need.

We must humbly and joyfully serve the body of Christ because God first served us by sacrificing His Son on the cross. We must love others more than ourselves, because that is how God showed His love to us. God loves the poor in Christ as much as the rest of us, and even more through His vindicating justice and the merciful and precious blood of His Son Jesus

Christ. Jesus selflessly spilled His own divine blood for the benefit of the whole church. Let us serve others the way our Lord served, and continues to serve, us.

*God's Promise:*
You were saved to serve the body of Christ with everything you have, for you are not your own.

# God's Sovereignty

> Let everyone be subject to the governing authorities, for there is no authority except that which God has established. The authorities that exist have been established by God. Consequently, whoever rebels against the authority is rebelling against what God has instituted, and those who do so will bring judgment on themselves.
>
> —Romans 13:1–2 (NIV)

We forget that God is sovereign and in control of everything. To yield to the authority placed over us is to honor God, for He alone is sovereign and in total control over the ways of man. There is no authority established that has not been established by God.

Children must obey and honor their parents. Wives must honor the authority of the husband who is subjected to the authority of Christ as the head of the church. And in all things, we must honor the authority of our local, state, and national leaders. God is in control. Obey God, then obey the authorities.

So much anger and hatred lies in our hearts for our nation's leaders, but this is ungodly and fuels unforgiveness and bitterness, which in turn blocks

God's blessing from our lives.[351] Who are we to question God's anointing of kings? God anointed Saul and many other evil kings over Israel and Judah. God's kings bring God's sovereign justice and rule to this earth, as well as salvation and peace.

When we rebel in our hearts against a president, for example, whether he is morally wrong or right for his decisions, we rebel against God. God brings prosperity and allows tribulation, all according to His divine justice and plan for salvation. Through prosperity, He brings blessings and peace to faithful and tired peoples. Through tribulation, He brings correction to a nation that kills over a million unborn babies a year and celebrates homosexuality.[352]

When a nation attacks another nation out of revenge in order to overthrow the king, instead of trusting God to bring justice, the result is years of spiritual famine under a new evil leader with tens of thousands of madmen running rampant in the stead of one. Revenge comes from unforgiveness, and if we refuse to forgive, God will not forgive us. If God does not forgive us, then judgment must follow.

Judgment comes when we rebel against God's anointed instead of praying for them. We must pray for the salvation of our leaders in this world and forgive them. Our comfort must be in God's promise that all authorities are established by God and under the sovereign rule of Jesus Christ, the one true King.

*God's Promise:*
The ways of kings sway in the wind according to the wishes of the Spirit of God.

# Love Is Everything

> Let no debt remain outstanding, except the continuing debt to love one another, for whoever loves others has fulfilled the law. The commandments, "You shall not commit adultery," "You shall not murder," "You shall not steal," "You shall not covet," and whatever other command there may be, are summed up in this one command: "Love your neighbor as yourself." Love does no harm to a neighbor. Therefore love is the fulfillment of the law.
>
> —Romans 13:8–10 (NIV)

Whoever loves fulfills the law. Whoever does not love, does not fulfill the law, is a lawbreaker, and sins. Whoever hates his brother, hates the law and the authority behind the law, which is God.

Love is absolutely essential to life and is our created purpose. God created us to love and to be loved. Love imagined us, spoke us into existence, gives us life, saved us on Calvary, and now reigns in us through the Holy Spirit.

We must love our worst enemies: those killing us like sheep with swords; those killing us with words;

those killing us in their hearts. Love = forgiveness.

Jesus gave up His life because He loved us so much it drove Him to forgive even the most evil amongst us. It is love that cried out on the cross, "Father, forgive them, for they do not know what they do," and that covers all of us.[353]

Let no debt go unforgiven in your heart. Jesus suffered to forgive a man's sin, and if we retain that same particular sin over them, a sin Jesus already paid for, we have, by our selfishness, made Jesus suffer for nothing, and we crucify Him all over again.[354]

To love means to forgive. To love means to do good to your neighbor. The Holy Spirit is our guide in what love looks like. If we are looking to love, we will love our neighbor first in our heart, which causes the angels of heaven to move on their behalf. If God desires us to act and stand in the gap for our neighbor, He will prompt us to act out our love, and always for our blessing and reward. Have only love in your heart for others, and the whole law is made perfect in you.

*God's Promise:*

Christ is love incarnate and now lives in us as the fulfillment of the law of love, faith, and obedience.

# Every Knee

> You, then, why do you judge your brother or sister? Or why do you treat them with contempt? For we will all stand before God's judgment seat. It is written: "'As surely as I live,' says the Lord, 'every knee will bow before me; every tongue will acknowledge God.'" So then, each of us will give an account of ourselves to God.
>
> —Romans 14:10–12 (NIV)

We must account for ourselves before God—the unbeliever, yes, but especially the believer. What we have done with this salvation we have been given and the love we have been shown will be weighed. Every word spoken, every message written, and every thought entertained had hopefully been created by the love for others we had emitting from our heart.[355]

Judgment belongs to the Lord. We have no right to judge anyone for anything.[356] The best we can do is to speak the truth as it is found in the Word of God to someone with love, tenderness, and humility.[357]

Christ has forgiven all sins on Calvary and beckons us to forgive in like manner. Because He lived with us, Jesus understands our sinful condition, human weakness, and limitations. We must love because Jesus loves. We must have compassion on others because Jesus had compassion on us. We must give grace to others because God leads us from grace to grace each moment of our lives. He supplies grace in opportunities to choose what is good and just. He supplies grace in opportunities to freely choose to love without consequence.

Every knee will bow for a very good reason, because on that Day, our lives will be intricately and immediately revealed to us. Each thought we had and how it affected our action or inaction; every word we spoke and whether it lifted others up or knocked them down—all will be revealed to us in either a sorrowful or joyful manner. Each of our choices will be clearly understood as to how they impacted others as seen through the perfect love of Jesus Christ.

No one will be able to deny their judgment before the throne of God because truth will be perfectly understood in the midst of Christ's righteousness, love, and justice. Each of us will judge ourselves before Christ as our lives are revealed, and every knee will bow by our own choice. We will submit to His love and either have a crown placed upon our head because of Christ's righteousness, or have nothing.

*God's Promise:*

In the presence of Christ's righteousness, every knee will bow as we examine our lives and choices in the light of God's love for mankind.

# Clean and Unclean

Therefore let us stop passing judgment on one another. Instead, make up your mind not to put any stumbling block or obstacle in the way of a brother or sister. I am convinced, being fully persuaded in the Lord Jesus, that nothing is unclean in itself. But if anyone regards something as unclean, then for that person it is unclean. If your brother or sister is distressed because of what you eat, you are no longer acting in love. Do not by your eating destroy someone for whom Christ died. Therefore do not let what you know is good be spoken of as evil. For the kingdom of God is not a matter of eating and drinking, but of righteousness, peace and joy in the Holy Spirit, because anyone who serves Christ in this way is pleasing to God and receives human approval. Let us therefore make every effort to do what leads to peace and to mutual edification. Do not destroy the work of God for the sake of food. All food is clean, but it is wrong for a person to eat anything that causes someone else to stumble. It is better not to eat meat or drink wine or to do anything else that will cause your brother or sister to fall. So whatever you believe about these things keep between yourself and God.

> Blessed is the one who does not condemn himself by what he approves. But whoever has doubts is condemned if they eat, because their eating is not from faith; and everything that does not come from faith is sin.
>
> —Romans 14:13–23 (NIV)

We are free in Christ to love. When we were saved, the kingdom of God came to us and now lives in us, on earth as it is in heaven.[358] God the Holy Spirit now takes up His living residence in our hearts.

We have been permanently cleaned by the ever-atoning blood of Christ. We must be perfectly clean always and forever for the Holy One to be able to live in us. There is nothing that we can put in our bodies, whether of food or drink or by sight or sound, that can make us clean. Likewise, there is nothing we can do to defile ourselves and become unclean, for the kingdom of God is not about what goes inside, but about Who is inside: the Holy Spirit. From within His temple, the kingdom of God is what comes out of us, and it is manifested by the peace, joy, and love we show toward our brothers and sisters in Christ.

There are two things that make something unclean. First, we can make something that is clean or unclean for us a stumbling block for others. If what we do causes our brother or sister to be wounded in their faith or walk in the Spirit, it is a grave error, and we effectually demonstrate hate for that person out of our carelessness or selfishness. In all we do, we must do it in love for our neighbor, lest we cause their salvation to be delayed by our poor Christian lifestyle or thwart their meeting God's divine will and spiritual growth due to our lack of edification.

God is persistently sanctifying each of us unto perfection in Christ Jesus, but many of our delays in growth are attributed to stumbling caused by people we love and respect who call themselves Christians. While it can and should be easy for us to forgive them, the damage done from their lack of sensitivity to our hearts can be permanent. We must ever be sensitive to the weaknesses and needs of others and lift them up in Christ and do nothing that may tear them down.[359]

With a simple example, take alcohol: we can destroy another's faith walk with God by our stance on alcohol. There are churches in America that won't let you be a member if you drink alcohol! But if you were raised in a German family, and knowing from the Bible that everything is clean in Christ, this "Christian" rule can be devastating. "How can a Christian church tell me I am going to hell and reject me for drinking a beer when the Bible says it is okay," the wounded Christian asks in his heart. This type of hypocrisy is what is driving many young Christians out of the churches today.

By taking an anti-alcohol stance, just because it is easy for you to resist and because it is unclean for you, making it a self-righteous law for yourself, and imposing it on others turns your personal belief into a dagger—the love of God is not seen in you, but rather a hatred for your brother or sister in Christ projects.[360]

This same self-righteous law sets yourself up for

great failure and disgrace before your brothers and sisters should you fall into your own self-made temptation and toast at a wedding celebration or in another way "slip up." If drinking alcohol is unclean for you, keep it to yourself and do it by faith to God as a sacrificial offering of service. Once your commitment to not drinking alcohol becomes a public display, pride and arrogance produces its fruit, and the kingdom of God is not seen in you.[361]

In similar manner, if drinking is clean to you, it is clean to God, if you drink without drunkenness and do it with self-control and in faith before God, submitting to His will and Spirit.[362] In all things, subjection to the will of God with humility is required. If you cannot have that beer or glass of wine in sincere thanks to God and feel clean about it because by faith you know it is approved of God for you, then it is unclean to you.

Anything that harms your relationship with God is unclean, and only you can know what is clean and unclean for your walk with the Lord; it is for this reason we have the Holy Spirit. He intricately teaches and sanctifies us to be like Christ and have peace and joy in Him.[363]

In Christ, our chains have been broken, and we have been set free from the law, the laws of man, and self-made laws. But being free does not mean we should not adhere to the laws of God and men, rather it is by following the law that we honor others and please God by being subject to the authorities and governments placed over us by God. We should be all things to all people such that some might be saved.

All things are clean, but not all things are profitable

to our walk with God,[364] and not all things help us fulfill our purpose in life, which is to love. If we do anything that causes a brother or sister to be hurt, we have broken the only remaining law of God, which is to love. To love like Jesus means to lift up, encourage, and be selfless in service with sacrifice for the sake of others at the expense of yourself.[365]

The second way to make something unclean is to make it a sin. We sin when we hide from God, desiring to be in the presence of the world and self rather than in the presence of God in righteousness.[366] If drinking beer causes us to become angry, insensitive, or reckless, these are good signs that drinking is unclean to us. It proves we did not do it in faith and did not display the kingdom of God by having peace and joy in the presence of the Holy Spirit living inside of us. But if we are praising God the whole time in songs of worship with uplifting speech, then for us, it may indeed be clean and a way for us to connect in a closer way with the presence of God; but this must be between you and God alone.

Be ever aware of not speaking this to others, because to them, this may destroy their faith placed in you and God! People by nature need others to look up to and inspire them to walk stronger in faith, and if your drinking, eating, or whatever you do that is clean to you by faith before God causes them to fall, it is better that you have a millstone tied around your neck and be drowned in the depths of the sea.[367]

Let your drinking be done in secret if you drink. Let your watching of violent movies be done in secret if you do it by faith. Let your listening to heavy metal music be done in secret if it is done by faith. While these are unclean for most Christians, whether they participate in such activities or not, it does not necessarily mean that it is unclean for you. Allow the Holy Spirit to be your guide and keep it between you and God. But remember, holiness is our goal and command, so be holy for God is holy and living inside of you, His holy temple cleansed by His own blood.

Do not do things before others without extreme care and sensitivity, because another may be greatly wounded by it, for to them it may be unclean, and they may never grow spiritually enough in this life to understand how it could also not be unclean to you, someone whom they have placed on a spiritual pedestal above themselves. Do not condemn yourself by what you approve. Do all things in love before others, and do all things in faith before God.

*God's Promise:*

Everything that does not come from faith is sin, and everything that comes from faith is clean if handled in love.

# Paul's Comfort

> For everything that was written in the past was written to teach us, so that through the endurance taught in the Scriptures and the encouragement they provide we might have hope. May the God of hope fill you with all joy and peace as you trust in him, so that you may overflow with hope by the power of the Holy Spirit.
>
> —Romans 15:4, 13 (NIV)

Saul knew the Scriptures as well as anyone. He was a Pharisee trained by the best, and he was zealous for the holy Scriptures. But for Saul, the Scriptures told him to persecute these radical followers of Jesus in the name of the God of the Jews. Saul's hope was in the sword, in pride, in money, and in a version of God that man created, but not in the Lord God.

All of the Scriptures were written for us, the church, so that when the Holy Spirit came to us, our eyes would be opened to see the faith of the Lord—His patience, purpose, and promises—fulfilled perfectly in the revelation of His mystery: Jesus Christ our Redeemer, High Priest, and King. The Scriptures were dead to most of the Jews because without the Spirit of God bringing them to life, man cannot discern spiritual things.[368]

When the Holy Spirit entered Saul, his eyes were opened, and his heart of stone was made into a heart of flesh, a heart that God could finally write His Word upon. Now Paul, a perfect version of Saul the stone, had a new hope, a new comfort: the Word of God.

Paul saw the Scriptures in a new light—as in a mirror, he saw God's purpose in it all: to save for Himself a people to whom He was proven faithful even as they rejected Him. Paul saw a God of hope: a God who would never leave nor forsake him; a God who saves because He promised it so and fulfilled all His promises in Christ Jesus.

We have this hope in jars of clay: Christ in us, the hope of glory.[369] This hope is perfect though, because Scriptures teach us that God is perfect in goodness and love, faithful to the test, and worthy to be praised and glorified.[370]

The Word is alive in us! The Holy Spirit comforts us as the Word shows us who God truly is and that He is faithful to His promises all the time. When we allow the Spirit of Christ to teach us through His Word, we are comforted in Jesus' presence and can fearlessly obey His commandments to love. Through this holy comfort—the comfort of our Holy Father—we are filled with joy and peace as we serve the Lord our God and Savior, Jesus Christ the Lord.

The purpose for our salvation here on earth is to carry on the work of the love of Jesus Christ until He returns. The Holy Spirit comforts us as we accomplish

His will in this fallen world. We have been saved to serve, and all the spiritual weapons needed to humbly serve Christ in love are provide by the Spirit for our comfort and assured victory.

*God's Promise:*
With the encouragement of the Word of endurance and the Spirit of hope, we can serve our Lord Jesus Christ with the comfort of His joy and peace, overflowing from within us, for the world God loves.

# Saved to Serve

> Now to him who is able to establish you in accordance with my gospel, the message I proclaim about Jesus Christ, in keeping with the revelation of the mystery hidden for long ages past, but now revealed and made known through the prophetic writings by the command of the eternal God, so that all the Gentiles might come to the obedience that comes from faith—to the only wise God be glory forever through Jesus Christ! Amen.
>
> —Romans 16:25–27 (NIV)

The mystery of the Gospel has been made known to those who have yielded their lives to the will of God. The mystery is Christ in us, the hope of glory.

The God of the universe has chosen you, cleaned your home, and taken up His residence inside of you to accomplish His work of saving mankind through you as His hands and feet. Your heart is to become the very heart of God for this fallen world, which He loves.

It is only through your obedience by faith that God can accomplish His purposes for your life. Without your trust, God cannot get the glory. And He is full of glory and rightly to be praised. He has commanded you to give your life back to Him by your own free will as a good and reasonable offering for the miraculous work He performed in you. It is a good thing to wholeheartedly serve the God who rescued you from death and gave you eternal life as joint heirs in the kingdom of the Son He loves.

God is in the process of sanctifying you in Christ and reconciling you to Him so that He can love and bless you for eternity. The miracle of this is that God is looking for kingdom-minded followers of Jesus to be willing vessels for His Son's work of salvation. God does not need our help to accomplish His work, yet He limits His efforts to require our help. He loves us so dearly, He wants us all to share in the victory Christ won on the cross without having to pay the penalty for our sin. What a good, good Father!

God is present in us with the Holy Spirit. His very life is living inside of us in order to give us the power, the ability, and the desire to partner with Him in what He is doing here on earth. This is the marvelous mystery of the Gospel! God desires a love relationship with you so that you can share in the joy and glory of His work of saving His children!

His call is the same to every Christian believer who has already accepted Christ as Savior. We have been saved to serve God. We are commanded to let go of this dying world and take hold of the life that is life: the life of Christ living inside of us!

Be obedient servants of our most high King. Seek His face and enter into a beautiful love relationship with Jesus. God has only good and perfect things planned for you. He saved you to serve Him. God designed you and gifted you for a specific task related to the Gospel.

He has saved you to sacrificially offer your life and gifts back to Him in order to bring Him glory and show this world the magnificent and immeasurable love of God through Jesus Christ our Savior.

Trust your God. Let Christ be your King. Let the Holy Spirit be your Comforter. Be obedient to the Gospel. Have faith in the promises of God.

*God's Promise:*

We have all been saved to serve the ones Jesus died to save because He first served us with His own life.

# Closing Thoughts

Paul's comfort changed the world. Isaiah prophesied Him,[371] the apostles received Him,[372] Paul experienced Him like never before, and the world has never been the same.

Paul's comfort was the very life and presence of God living inside of him, giving him strength, love, peace, joy, and hope, in times of prosperity and in times of tribulation. The promises of God never failed Paul, they have never failed any of those who belong to Jesus Christ, and they will never fail you.

My prayer is that you would be ever reminded of the overflowing and overwhelming love of God through the manifestation of His power and grace administered by Holy Spirit through the living Word. The promises of God are alive and can be alive in you as you trust and obey His commandments and live by faith, not by sight.

The Bible is true, and His Word never fails, for the Holy Spirit of God sees to it that every word in it comes to pass with truth and power. Have childlike faith in the promises of God, and the extraordinary life will be yours today, tomorrow, and for all of eternity.

May the Lord bless you and keep you; may He shine His face upon you; may He lift His countenance toward you, and give you peace, in Jesus's name. Amen.

# Endnotes

[1] Isaiah 14:12; Exodus 34:5–7; 1 John 4:8; Job 1:6–12; Job 2:1–6; Matthew 4:1–11; Genesis 3:14–15.
[2] Luke 10:18.
[3] James 4:17.
[4] 1 John 2:2.
[5] John 3:16.
[6] 1 John 1:5.
[7] 2 Chronicles 7:1-3.
[8] Genesis 1:27; Acts 17:24–31; Romans 2:12–16.
[9] 1 Timothy 5:24.
[10] Romans 11:5–6; Isaiah 28:5; Psalm 74:2; Revelation 5:9.
[11] John 3:16–17; Romans 6:23; Romans 10:9.
[12] Matthew 18:14; John 12:47; 1 Timothy 4:10.
[13] 1 Corinthians 12:27; Ephesians 3:6; Colossians 1:24.
[14] John 13:34–35.
[15] 1 Corinthians 6:20; 1 Corinthians 7:23.
[16] Ephesians 6:6; Galatians 5:25; Romans 6:11.
[17] Galatians 5:16.
[18] 2 Peter 1:19–21; 2 Timothy 3:16–17.
[19] Luke 12:33; Luke 18:22; 1 Corinthians 13:3.
[20] Galatians 6:14.
[21] Acts 13:47; Matthew 28:19–20; 1 John 2:4.
[22] John 12:44; John 14:9–12; John 17:20–23.
[23] John 5:24.
[24] 2 Corinthians 10:4–5; Ephesians 3:14–20; Colossians 1:9–14.
[25] Matthew 6:33; Philippians 4:19.
[26] John 14:12–14.
[27] John 13:34–35; Romans 12:1, 9–13, 20.
[28] Galatians 2:20; Colossians 1:29.

29 Isaiah 9:6; Isaiah 57:21; Acts 10:36; Romans 5:1–2; Romans 15:33; Romans 16:20; 1 Corinthians 14:33; Philippians 4:7; 1 Thessalonians 5:23; Hebrews 13:20; 2 John 1:3.
30 2 Corinthians 12:9.
31 Colossians 1:19–20; Colossians 2:13–15.
32 Lamentations 3:22–23.
33 2 Corinthians 6:1–2.
34 Ephesians 6:10–17.
35 John 3:6; Romans 8:5, 13.
36 Galatians 5:16–17.
37 Romans 5:1–2.
38 2 Corinthians 1:3–7.
39 Jeremiah 8:18; John 14:16–17, 26; John 15:26; John 16:7.
40 1 Peter 2:24.
41 Isaiah 25:6–8; Revelation 21:3–4.
42 Galatians 4:6–7.
43 Psalm 86:12–13.
44 Romans 8:1.
45 1 Corinthians 12:12–13.
46 John 16:8–11.
47 Acts 26:17–18; 1 Corinthians 1:2.
48 Matthew 5:48; Matthew 19:21; 2 Corinthians 12:9–10; Hebrews 10:14.
49 Acts 9:17–19.
50 Ephesians 2:1–5.
51 Acts 9:15–16.
52 2 Corinthians 8:9; 2 Corinthians 11:24–27.
53 John 13:34.
54 Acts 1:8.
55 Matthew 28:19–20.
56 2 Corinthians 1:6.
57 Acts 17:26; Daniel 2:21; John 15:16.
58 Luke 12:25; Matthew 6:27.
59 Jeremiah 17:10; Jeremiah 32:19; Proverbs 12:14; Proverbs 14:14; Psalm 17:14; Matthew 6:2, 5, 16.

[60] 1 Chronicles 28:9; Psalm 139:17–18; Matthew 10:30; Luke 12:7.
[61] John 17:3.
[62] 1 Timothy 6:18–19.
[63] Matthew 10:38; Matthew 16:24; Mark 8:34; Mark 10:21; Luke 14:27; Luke 18:22.
[64] Acts 9:3, 7–9.
[65] Acts 9:20.
[66] John 10:9; Ephesians 1:11–14; 2 Corinthians 1:21–22; 2 Corinthians 5:5.
[67] Romans 8:29–30; Ephesians 1:3–10.
[68] Ephesians 4:11–14; 1 Corinthians 3:1–3; Hebrews 5:11–14.
[69] Ezekiel 11:19; Ezekiel 36:26; 2 Corinthians 3:3.
[70] Luke 1:68–75.
[71] Acts 8:1–3; Acts 9:1–3.
[72] https://www.opendoorsusa.org/, accessed December 20, 2014; http://www.prisoneralert.com/, accessed December 20, 2014; http://www.christianpersecution.info/, accessed December 20, 2014; http://www. persecution.com/, accessed December 20, 2014.
[73] Matthew 5:21–22; Matthew 15:19; Mark 7:20–22; 1 John 3:15.
[74] Luke 4:28–29.
[75] Acts 22:12-16.
[76] Matthew 28:19.
[77] 1 Thessalonians 1:4–6; 2 Timothy 3:16–17; Jeremiah 31:33; Hebrews 8:10; Hebrews 10:16.
[78] Matthew 13:3-7.
[79] Ezekiel 12:25; Matthew 24:25; Mark 13:31; Luke 21:33; Hebrews 4:12.
[80] Romans 10:14.
[81] 2 Corinthians 1:20.
[82] Psalm 34:8; 1 Peter 2:2–3.
[83] Romans 14:17–18.
[84] Romans 15:24–28; 1 Clement 5:7.

[85] References:
(1) http://asis.com/users/stag/paulbrit.html, accessed December 22, 2014;
(2) http://israelect.com/ChildrenOfYahweh/Campbell/lost_chapter.htm, accessed December 22, 2014.

[86] Acts 19:21; Acts 23:11.

[87] James Stalker, *The Life of St. Paul* (New York: Revell), © 1912 American Tract Society, p.10, Kindle edition.

[88] James Stalker, *The Life of St. Paul* (New York: Revell), © 1912 American Tract Society, p.12, Kindle edition.

[89] 1 Corinthians 13:8.

[90] Romans 15:18.

[91] Colossians 3:3.

[92] Reference: "The Letters of Paul," http://www.systematicchristianity.org/TheLettersOfPaul.htm, accessed 3-12-2014, last modified 8-28-2011.

[93] Matthew McGee, "Chronology of Apostle Paul's Journeys and Epistles," http://www.matthewmcgee.org/paultime.html, accessed 3-12-2014.

[94] James Stalker, *The Life of St. Paul* (New York: Revell), © 1912 American Tract Society, p.13, Kindle edition.

[95] The final order of this study was developed mathematically by strength of chronological reference for 1 Thessalonians through Philemon. The final order of Hebrews, 1 Timothy, Titus, and 2 Timothy order was set because most scholars agree to this order.

| Epistle | Date[1] | Location[2] | Order[3] |
|---|---|---|---|
| 1 Thess. | 52 | Corinth | 1.3 |
| 2 Thess. | 52 | Corinth | 2.4 |
| Galatians | 55-57 | Ephesus | 3.2 |
| 1 Corinth. | 57 | Ephesus | 3.5 |
| 2 Corinth. | 57 | Ephesus | 4.8 |
| Romans | 57-58 | Corinth | 5.8 |
| Ephesians | 62 | Rome | 7.3 |

| Colossians | 62 | Rome | 7.4 |
| Philippians | 62 | Rome | 7.6 |
| Philemon | 63 | Rome | 7.7 |
| Hebrews | 64-65 | Rome | 11 |
| 1 Timothy | 64-65 | Macedonia | 12 |
| Titus | 64-65 | Greece | 13 |
| 2 Timothy | 66-67 | Rome | 14 |

(1) The approximate dates are taken from http://www.matthewmcgee.org/paultime.html, last accessed December 24, 2014, and are for general reference only.

(2) The estimated locations (except for Hebrews) are taken from http://www.bombaxo.com/paulchron.html, last accessed December 24, 2014, and are for general reference only.

(3) Each book was given an order number from each the following references, and the average order was calculated to determine the final order of this study, all accessed March 17, 2014:
  i. http://www.bombaxo.com/paulchron.html
  ii. http://www.matthewmcgee.org/paultime.html
  iii. http://www.blueletterbible.org/study/paul/timeline.cfm
  iv. http://www.systematicchristianity.org/TheLettersOfPaul.htm
  v. http://www.featheredprop.com/?page_id=71
  vi. http://www.biblestudytools.com/commentaries/scofield-reference-notes/pauline-epistles.html, also http://www.christianity.com/bible/books-of-the-bible/the-epistles-of-paul-11541689.html
  vii. http://www.foundationsforfreedom.net/References/NT/Pauline/Pauline_Letters-Chronology.html
  viii. http://www.angelfire.com/nv/TheOliveBranch/append192.html
  ix. http://lists.ibiblio.org/pipermail/corpus-paul/19990330/000029.html
  x. http://www.heavendwellers.com/hd_aa_chronology_acts_and_epist.htm

[96] John 3:15; John 6:47.
[97] Romans 8:11.
[98] Luke 15:10.
[99] 1 Thessalonians 1:4–6; Romans 8:5–6.
[100] Ephesians 2:8; 2 Timothy 1:9.
[101] Hebrews 3:14.
[102] 1 Thessalonians 5:19; Galatians 6:8.
[103] Revelation 19:7–9; Revelation 2:1–5.
[104] 1 Corinthians 12:27; Ephesians 4:15.
[105] Revelation 2:23.
[106] Revelation 20:11–15.
[107] 2 Corinthians 2:15.
[108] Acts 26:17–18.
[109] Proverbs 8:13.
[110] 1 Corinthians 2:15–16; Philippians 4:7.
[111] Matthew 12:28; John 3:3–5; Mark 9:1; Acts 1:3; Romans 14:17; 1 Corinthians 4:20.
[112] 1 Peter 5:4.
[113] 2 Timothy 4:8; James 1:12; Psalm 103:4.
[114] Matthew 6:19–20.
[115] 1 Peter 1:1–3.
[116] 1 Peter 1:15–16.
[117] Romans 12:9.
[118] Romans 8:1–2.
[119] Proverbs 20:13.
[120] Acts 26:14.
[121] Luke 12:46.
[122] Psalm 96:13; Romans 8:19–22.
[123] Matthew 8:12; Matthew 13:42; Luke 13:27–28.
[124] Psalm 85:2; Colossians 2:13–14.
[125] Galatians 5:1.
[126] 1 Peter 2:16; James 1:25; James 2:12.
[127] Ephesians 1:3–5.
[128] Genesis 2:7; Job 33:4.
[129] Romans 7:5.
[130] 1 Corinthians 6:20; 1 Corinthians 7:23.
[131] Romans 6:23.

[132] 1 John 3:10.
[133] 2 Corinthians 12:9.
[134] Romans 3:27.
[135] James 2:14–26.
[136] Ephesians 1:5–6.
[137] Isaiah 64:6.
[138] Romans 8:7; James 4:4.
[139] Romans Chapter 7.
[140] Ephesians 6:18.
[141] Genesis 2:16–17; Genesis 5:5; Psalm 88:3.
[142] Ezra 9:13.
[143] Psalm 119:156; Psalm 145:8–9; Lamentations 3:22–23.
[144] Ephesians 2:3.
[145] Romans 8:28.
[146] Romans 8:37.
[147] 1 John 3:16.
[148] Matthew 23:23–36.
[149] John 21:25.
[150] Psalm 139:17–18.
[151] Matthew 4:1.
[152] Romans 12:1.
[153] John 6:37.
[154] 1 John 4:8.
[155] John 3:16.
[156] Psalm 7:11; Psalm 58:11; Romans 2:16; Hebrews 4:12.
[157] 1 Corinthians 15:1–2.
[158] 2 Corinthians 6:1.
[159] Mark 16:9; Acts 10:41.
[160] Acts 1:3.
[161] John 9:4.
[162] Revelation 22:12.
[163] 2 Corinthians 5:1.
[164] 1 Peter 2:9; Ephesians 1:11–12; Ephesians 2:10; Philippians 2:12–13.
[165] John 15:5.

[166] John 15:6; Galatians 5:13, 16.
[167] John 15:19.
[168] 1 Corinthians 16:14.
[169] 2 Corinthians 11:24–28.
[170] Acts 16:22–25.
[171] Matthew 27:46; Mark 15:34.
[172] 1 Peter 3:14; Acts 9:16; Romans 5:3; Romans 8:17–18; Colossians 1:24.
[173] Hebrews 4:14.
[174] Matthew 6:33; Psalm 16:2; Psalm 84:11.
[175] 1 Corinthians 1:30; 2 Corinthians 7:1; Romans 6:22; Ephesians 4:30.
[176] Hebrews 13:5.
[177] Matthew 4:4; Luke 11:28; Hebrews 1:1–2; Hebrews 4:12; John 1:1.
[178] Hebrews 10:15–16; 1 John 5:6; Revelation 1:1–2.
[179] Job Chapter 41; Psalm 104.
[180] Acts 10:36.
[181] John 14:21.
[182] Matthew 10:38; Mark 8:34; Luke 9:23; John 10:27.
[183] Mark 10:21; Luke 18:22.
[184] 1 John 4:19.
[185] Romans 6:23.
[186] John 8:12.
[187] Romans 8:15; 2 Corinthians 7:1; 2 Timothy 1:7; Romans 15:13; Galatians 5:5; Ephesians 4:4.
[188] Matthew 10:39; Matthew 16:25; Mark 8:35; Luke 9:24; Luke 17:33; John 12:25.
[189] Hebrews 12:1-3.
[190] Job 3:25–26; Isaiah 59:2, 8.
[191] Isaiah 52:7; Acts 10:36.
[192] 1 Corinthians 12:13.
[193] Proverbs 3:5–6; Psalm 9:1; Psalm 62:8; Psalm 86:12; Psalm 119:10; Psalm 138:1; Jeremiah 29:13; Joel 2:12; Matthew 22:37; Mark 12:30–33; Luke 10:27.

[194] Colossians 3:23; Galatians 2:20.
[195] James 4:17.
[196] Matthew 16:24; John 12:26; John 21:19.
[197] Matthew 24:45–51; Matthew 25:14–30.
[198] Romans 8:11.
[199] Colossians 2:6; 1 John 3:16; Ephesians 4:1.
[200] John 7:17; John 15:16; James 4:4.
[201] 2 Timothy 4:9–10.
[202] Romans 1:20.
[203] Matthew 10:38; Matthew 25:46.
[204] Matthew 6:24.
[205] 1 Thessalonians 1:5.
[206] Luke 6:35; Matthew 19:21.
[207] John 15:19.
[208] 1 Thessalonians 4:3; 1 Thessalonians 5:23; 1 Peter 1:1–2; Romans 8:23; Philippians 3:21.
[209] Romans Chapter 7.
[210] Mark 14:58; Acts 17:24; 1 Corinthians 3:16; 1 Corinthians 6:19.
[211] Matthew 26:41; Mark 14:38.
[212] John 17:19.
[213] Matthew 4:1.
[214] Hebrews 10:24–25.
[215] John 17:11, 21.
[216] John 16:33; Matthew 13:21; Mark 4:17; 2 Corinthians 1:3–5.
[217] Matthew 6:8.
[218] Luke 11:13.
[219] Romans 4:19–21; Colossians 2:6–7.
[220] John 8:32.
[221] John 18:37.
[222] 1 Corinthians 12:11.
[223] 1 Peter 5:8.
[224] Galatians 5:7–8.
[225] Proverbs 8:12–17.
[226] Hebrews 4:12–13; Revelation 1:16.

[227] Ephesians 2:1–10.
[228] Ephesians 6:17.
[229] 1 Corinthians 2:2; 2 Thessalonians 1:12.
[230] 1 John 1:8.
[231] Romans 8:10–11.
[232] Acts 17:28; Colossians 2:6–7; 1 John 3:24.
[233] 1 John 5:16–20.
[234] 1 John 2:1.
[235] 1 Corinthians 10:13.
[236] John 1:29; 2 Corinthians 5:18–19; Hebrews 4:3; Hebrews 9:26; 1 John 2:2.
[237] Colossians 3:23–24; Hebrews 9:15; 1 Peter 1:3–5.
[238] Matthew 18:16; 2 Corinthians 13:1; 1 Timothy 5:19; 2 Timothy 3:16–17.
[239] Colossians 2:9–10.
[240] 1 Thessalonians 4:2; Titus 2:15.
[241] 1 Corinthians 2:2.
[242] Matthew 5:16; Ephesians 4:1; Colossians 1:9–10; 1 Thessalonians 2:12.
[243] Romans 3:22; Romans 5:17; Romans 8:10; Romans 10:4; 1 Corinthians 1:30; Galatians 2:21; Philippians 1:11; Philippians 3:9; 2 Peter 1:1.
[244] Romans 8:1–4.
[245] Romans 9:33; Romans 10:11.
[246] Romans 12:2; 2 Corinthians 3:18; Philippians 3:20–21.
[247] 1 Thessalonians 2:13; 1 Peter 1:23; 1 John 2:14; Hebrews 4:12.
[248] James 2:14–26; Hebrews Chapter 11.
[249] Psalm 85:10–11.
[250] 1 Corinthians 1:18.
[251] Galatians 5:13; 1 John 3:16; 1 John 4:21.
[252] Matthew 22:39; Mark 12:31, 33; Luke 10:27; Romans 13:9; Galatians 5:14; James 2:8.
[253] Luke 6:47; John 20:23; Acts 10:43; 1 John 2:12.
[254] 1 Thessalonians 4:7; 2 Timothy 1:9; 1 Peter 1:15–16.

## The Promises of God

[255] Exodus 34:6; Numbers 14:18; Nehemiah 9:17; Psalm 86:15; Psalm 103:8; Psalm 145:8; Joel 2:13; Jonah 4:2; Habakkuk 3:2.
[256] Matthew 6:11; Luke 9:23.
[257] The current murder rate of Christians because of their faith in Jesus Christ is reliably reported at an average of 255 per month at https://www.opendoorsusa.org/christian-persecution/, last accessed on September 14, 2018.
[258] Ephesians 2:8–9.
[259] Mark 5:34; 1 Corinthians 7:22; Ephesians 3:12; Revelation 1:4–6.
[260] Mark 10:18; Luke 18:19; Romans 3:12.
[261] Proverbs 8:13; Ecclesiastes 3:19.
[262] Matthew 5:20.
[263] John 11:43.
[264] Galatians 2:15–16; Matthew 7:15–23.
[265] Romans 7:7.
[266] Genesis 1:27.
[267] Psalm 103:11–12.
[268] Romans 8:26–27.
[269] Proverbs 10:16.
[270] 2 Corinthians 5:1–5.
[271] Philippians 3:20–21.
[272] Romans 5:10; Colossians 1:21–22.
[273] Romans 6:23.
[274] Genesis 2:17; Genesis 3:6; Genesis 5:5.
[275] Exodus 20:12; 1 Corinthians 15:56; Ephesians 6:1–3; Colossians 3:20.
[276] James 4:17; Romans 3:22–24.
[277] 2 Chronicles 7:1–3.
[278] 1 Thessalonians 3:8–9.
[279] Genesis 2:7; Job 12:10; Job 27:3; Job 33:4; Isaiah 42:5.
[280] Romans 7:14–25.
[281] Genesis 2:15.
[282] Genesis 3:1.

[283] John 1:29.
[284] Hebrews 9:26; 1 John 2:2.
[285] Galatians 3:13.
[286] James 4:17.
[287] 1 John 2:2.
[288] Revelation 1:18; Revelation 20:14.
[289] Matthew 27:51–53.
[290] Isaiah 26:11; Jeremiah 5:21; Matthew 13:13; 1 Corinthians 2:14.
[291] Luke 24:49; John 16:7.
[292] John 14:26; 1 Corinthians 12:7–11.
[293] Revelation 5:9.
[294] Ephesians 6:6; 1 Corinthians 6:11.
[295] Romans 7:25; Galatians 5:16.
[296] Galatians 3:13.
[297] Matthew 12:40; Matthew 27:63; Mark 14:58.
[298] Philippians 3:9.
[299] Romans 8:35–39.
[300] Deuteronomy 33:27; Jeremiah 10:10; Galatians 2:20; 1 John 5:20; Jude 1:20–21.
[301] John 15:1–16.
[302] John 16:7–11.
[303] 2 Corinthians 12:9.
[304] Matthew 3:8–9; Matthew 4:17; Mark 1:15; Mark 2:17; Luke 15:7, 10; Luke 17:3–4; Acts 2:38; Acts 3:19; Acts 5:31; 2 Corinthians 7:9–11; 2 Peter 3:9; Revelation 2:5.
[305] Hebrews 4:15.
[306] John 17:17; 1 Thessalonians 5:23.
[307] Romans 5:1–2; Colossians 1:27.
[308] Genesis 2:16–17.
[309] James 4:17.
[310] Isaiah 64:6.
[311] John 18:14.
[312] Psalm 14:1–3; Psalm 53:1–3; Romans 3:10–12.
[313] Ephesians 4:22–24.

[314] Ephesians 4:7.
[315] Deuteronomy 31:6–8; Hebrews 13:5.
[316] 1 Corinthians 1:30.
[317] Matthew 5:48; Hebrews 10:14.
[318] John 15:5, 16.
[319] 1 Corinthians 12:27; Ephesians 4:16; Romans 12:3–8.
[320] 1 Corinthians 3:16–23.
[321] Matthew 23:12; Luke 4:11; Luke 18:14; James 4:6, 10; 1 Peter 5:5–6.
[322] Luke 15:31; Matthew 7:7–11; Luke 11:8–13; John 15:16; John 16:23.
[323] James 1:5; Matthew 7:7; Luke 11:13.
[324] 2 Corinthians 7:1.
[325] Ephesians 1:5, 11; 1 Peter 1:1–2.
[326] Matthew 27:46; Mark 15:34; Hebrews 13:5.
[327] Matthew 6:33–34.
[328] Matthew 4:19; Matthew 16:24; Matthew 19:28; Mark 1:17; Mark 10:21; Luke 18:22; John 8:12; John 12:26.
[329] John 19:30.
[330] 2 Corinthians 1:21–22; 2 Corinthians 5:5.
[331] John 10:28.
[332] John 14:20.
[333] John 3:16; Luke 19:41–42; 2 Corinthians 2:15; 1 Peter 2:11–12; 2 Peter 3:9.
[334] James 4:10; Proverbs 22:4; Zephaniah 2:3; 1 Peter 5:5.
[335] Joshua 24:15; Deuteronomy 13:4; 1 Samuel 12:20; 2 Chronicles 19:9; Psalm 2:11; Matthew 4:10; Luke 4:8.
[336] Isaiah 29:16; Isaiah 45:9; Isaiah 64:8; Jeremiah 18:6; Lamentations 4:2; Romans 9:21.
[337] Job 38:4.
[338] Genesis 3:19; Genesis 18:27; Ecclesiastes 3:20; 1 Corinthians 13:2; 2 Corinthians 12:11.
[339] Acts 1:8; Acts 10:36; Acts 13:47.
[340] Ephesians 1:18.

[341] Matthew 5:44; Matthew 22:39; Mark 12:31–33; Luke 10:27; Romans 13:9; Galatians 5:14; James 2:8.
[342] John 13:34–35.
[343] Matthew 28:18–20; Acts 1:8.
[344] Hosea 4:6; Job 36:11–12; 1 Peter 5:8.
[345] John 15:8.
[346] Ephesians 2:1–3; Matthew 6:24; Luke 16:13; Joshua 24:15; 2 Kings 17:12; Psalm 106:36; Exodus 20:3; Matthew 6:21; Luke 12:34.
[347] 2 Corinthians 10:5.
[348] Luke 11:13; John 3:6; John 6:63; John 14:13–14; John 16:23–24; John 12:44; John 14:12.
[349] Matthew 6:33.
[350] Acts 20:28.
[351] Psalm 109:16–17; Proverbs 10:6; Proverbs 11:25–27.
[352] References:
  (1) http://www.operationrescue.org/about-abortion/abortions-in-america/, accessed September 23, 2018;
  (2) http://www.abort73.com/abortion_facts/us_abortion_statistics/, accessed September 23, 2018;
  (3) https://www.cnn.com/2015/06/26/politics/white-house-rainbow-marriage/index.html, accessed September 23, 2018.
[353] Luke 23:34
[354] John 20:23; Matthew 18:18; Matthew 6:14-15; Mark 11:25-26; Matthew 18:35; Luke 6:37.
[355] Matthew 5:22; Matthew 12:36.
[356] Matthew 7:1–2.
[357] Luke 17:3; Proverbs 15:32; Matthew 18:15.
[358] Matthew 6:9–10.
[359] 1 Thessalonians 5:11.
[360] Hebrews 5:12–14.
[361] Matthew 6:16–17.
[362] Galatians 5:22–24.

[363] Psalm 25:8–10.
[364] 1 Corinthians 6:12; 1 Corinthians 10:23.
[365] 1 Corinthians Chapter 13.
[366] Genesis 3:9.
[367] Matthew 18:6; Mark 9:32; Luke 17:2.
[368] 1 Corinthians 2:7, 14; 2 Corinthians 4:3–4; Romans 16:25; Ephesians 3:8–11; Colossians 1:25–27.
[369] 2 Corinthians 4:7; Romans 5:1–2.
[370] Psalm 18:3, 30; Psalm 48:1; Psalm 89:8; Psalm 96:4; Psalm 145:3; Deuteronomy 7:9; Deuteronomy 32:4; 2 Samuel 22:4, 31; 1 Chronicles 16:25; Mark 10:18; Luke 18:19; 1 John 4:8; 1 Corinthians 1:9; Revelation 5:12.
[371] Isaiah 44:3; Isaiah 59:21.
[372] Acts 2:1–4.

Made in the USA
Middletown, DE
07 November 2024